Other Books by the Authors

BUT IF NOT, VOLUME I

BUT IF NOT, VOLUME II

JESUS WEPT

LOSS AND GRIEF RECOVERY

8/5/11

Dear SKYLER & Lindsey,

But If Not

Congratulations !!

marriage Helps

P. 93   :)

Joyce & Dennis
Ashton

But If Not

COPING WITH UNEXPECTED LOSS

Volume Three

Joyce and Dennis Ashton

CFI
Springville, Utah

ISBN 13: 978-1-59955-270-5

Published by CFI, an imprint of Cedar Fort, Inc., 2373 W. 700 S., Springville, UT 84663
Distributed by Cedar Fort, Inc., www.cedarfort.com

LIBRARY OF CONGRESS CATALOGING-IN-PUBLICATION DATA

Ashton, Joyce.
 But if not : coping with unexpected loss / Joyce and
Dennis Ashton.
 p. cm.
 ISBN 978-1-59955-270-5
 1. Suffering—Religious aspects—Church of Jesus Christ of Latter-day
Saints. 2. Suffering—Religious aspects—Mormon Church. I. Ashton, Dennis,
1950- II. Title.

 BX8643.S93A83 2008
 248.8'6—dc22

                         2008010772

Cover design by Angela D. Olsen
Cover design © 2009 by Lyle Mortimer
Edited by Natalie A. Hepworth

Printed in the United States of America

10 9 8 7 6 5 4 3 2 1

Printed on acid-free paper

IN MEMORY OF

Our three youngest children,

ANDREW, BRANDON, AND ASHLEY,
WHO MAKE US PROUD AS THEY ENDURE THEIR
INDIVIDUAL LIFE CHALLENGES WITH
FAITH AND HOPE.

CONTENTS

Preface

Life is full of challenges, loss, and disappointment. The "But if Not" series is designed as a guide to help you manage and find meaning in your personal   tragedies. In Volume I, we explore helpful techniques and strategies to help you better cope and endure. We identify the unique grief symptoms and interventions available that will allow you to heal emotionally, spiritually, physically, socially, and intellectually. Volume II provides specific information and direction for those enduring disabilities, physical and mental illness, and coping with the death of a loved one. This current volume (III), addresses other unexpected losses that can bring pain and suffering. Of course we can't address every possible challenge one might experience; however, we do discuss addictions, abuse, divorce, rebellious children, children's grief, early returning missionaries, unwed pregnancies, infertility, adoption, never being married, empty nest, aging, and same-gender attraction.

We learned about loss and grief early in our marriage.

Our suffering and loss began with infertility, followed by the death of our first full-term baby daughter shortly after her birth. We started writing about grief many years later after experiencing the death of our disabled fourteen-year-old son, Cameron. Additional losses and life challenges have inevitability continued to roll into our family's life, including miscarriage, disabilities, death, addictions, physical and mental illness, and other more common challenges and adjustments. If we include our extended family, it covers every loss we have written about.

Inspiration for our grief series comes from a scripture passage found in Daniel 3:18, that includes the phrase "but if not." This scriptural sound bite gave us hope and comfort as we coped with the chronic illness of our oldest adult son, Darren, for a season. We knew God could deliver Darren, "but if not," we would choose to carry on and continue to be faithful and serve God. We wish you ultimate happiness and comfort on your life's journey. It is our hope and prayer that our stories, techniques, and spiritual insights will, in some beneficial way, ease your suffering and help you find meaning in your loss.

—Joyce and Dennis Ashton

CHAPTER ONE

But If Not

We are sorry your life's circumstances have brought you to a point where you are reading a book on loss. You probably didn't expect that these kinds of events would happen to you or your loved one and that your life would turn out quite this way. Your assumptive world has been assaulted.[1] You may struggle for some time to understand just what has happened and why.

Perhaps your pain and disappointment came to you early in life. Perhaps you experienced sexual or verbal abuse as a child. Perhaps you struggle with addiction or live with someone who does. Your daughter may have become pregnant out of wedlock; or your husband has left you for another woman, or even another man. Maybe you are currently experiencing emotional or spiritual abuse.

Perhaps your parents still got divorced even after you prayed, went on a mission, and placed their names on the prayer roll at the temple. Perhaps after years of infertility and miscarriages, you struggled to adopt a child. It could be that your full-time church mission ended before the appointed time in spite of your sincere efforts to overcome unrelenting anxiety and chronic depression. Maybe you have stayed in a difficult marriage in spite of intense marital discord. Perhaps you are divorced or have never married, and are wondering if this is how you will live out your earthy life. What if the joy of parenting has turned into a nightmare as you deal with difficult or rebellious children that rob you of emotional and financial reserves? Or you may struggle with aging and the secondary losses that accompany those "golden years." Others struggle with "empty nest syndrome" as they watch their children grow up and move away. Any of these significant life challenges and losses can leave you with heartache, disappointment, and grief. (If your loss comes as a result of disability, physical or mental illness, or the death of a loved one see *But if Not . . . Volume II.*)

After Dennis and I were married, we were asked by several young women groups to come and talk about our courtship and how we came to choose a temple marriage. They requested that I wear my wedding dress and tell the girls how exciting and beautiful our temple marriage was. The goal of the young women leaders was to persuade the girls to live righteous lives so they could go to the temple and live "happily ever after." Some years later in

California, a stake put on one such event. At the conclusion of the beautiful talks, including those given by a handsome bride and groom glowing in love, the stake president stood up. He said how wonderful the evening had been. After thanking everyone that participated, he said that he felt it was important that evening to also share some of life's potential tragic realities. He told the girls that evening that even if they kept the commandments and made few mistakes, it would not ensure that they would obtain a temple marriage. He told them some would never marry, some would marry and divorce, and some would experience devastating trials. He explained that the gospel was not an insurance policy to happiness and bliss. Dennis and I soon found his words to be accurate in our lives, as we experienced infertility followed by the death of our first full-term baby daughter. Our third child was born with cerebral palsy and spent his 14 years of life in a wheelchair. Other children came with learning disabilities, mental illnesses, and addictions. We have learned how quickly life can leave us as we buried both sets of parents (one at age 50 and one at age 61).

As we have tried to face and cope with each trial through the years, we have found lasting comfort in the scriptures. The scripture in Daniel 3:18 was especially helpful as we struggled with the critical illness of our oldest son, Darren. As an adult, he had a colon mass removed. Unfortunately, his surgery resulted in severe complications that required several additional surgeries over a two-year period. Through his suffering we came to more deeply appreciate a phrase from a favorite scripture that we quote to each other when one of us gets discouraged: "but if not . . ." The scriptures describe a powerful story about three virtuous and brave men. Shadrach, Meshach, and Abed-nego were told that they would be thrown into a "burning fiery furnace" if they continued worshipping their God. In spite of the inevitable consequences of their choice they chose not to bow down and worship King Nebuchadnezzar's golden image. They displayed their commitment and faith by responding: "Our God whom we serve is able to deliver us . . . *but if not*, be it known . . . that we will not serve thy gods, nor worship the golden image" (Daniel 3:18; emphasis added). We knew God could deliver Darren from his suffering, but if not we would continue to believe in and serve God.

Maybe you have experienced spiritual injury as a result of your loss. Maybe you have fasted and prayed for your situation to change, hoping for a miracle. Many faithful individuals do not receive the miracle they sincerely and desperately seek.

We may have been falsely taught that if we are righteous and faithful, we can avoid serious pain and loss. The scriptures confirm the reality that bad things happen to good people.[2] God "maketh his sun to rise on the evil and on the good, and sendeth rain on the just and on the unjust" (Matthew 5:45). Some endure pain as a result of the misuse of agency or the destructive and sometimes sinful choices of others. The scriptures also give ample evidence that good people must endure hard times. (For spiritual injury and healing, see Volume I.)

God may not remove our adversity, just as He didn't immediately deliver Alma and his people who were persecuted by Amulon. Instead, in Mosiah 24:14, He said, "I will ease the burdens which are put upon your shoulders, that even you cannot feel them on your backs." Alma the Younger, in Alma 31, discouraged with his preaching, prayed "that [he] may have strength, that [he] may suffer with patience these afflictions" (Alma 31:31). Even Christ felt forsaken and alone in Gethsemane. When He found His apostles asleep, He asked them, "Could ye not watch with me but one hour?" (Matthew 26:37). And later on the cross He asked His Father, "Why hast thou forsaken me?" (Matthew 27:46). We too may have feelings of being forsaken when we don't receive a miracle healing or when the Lord doesn't remove our adversity.

There may be times when our family and friends disappoint us by not supporting us in the way we think they should. We may have to accomplish some of our "Gethsemane work" without them. Neal A. Maxwell said of such suffering:

> There is, in the suffering of the highest order, a point reached—a point of aloneness—when the individual (as did the Savior on a much grander scale) must bear it, as it were, alone. Even the faithful may wonder if they can take any more or if they are in some way forsaken. Those who, as it were, stand at the foot of the cross, often can do so little to help absorb the pain and the anguish. It is something we must bear by ourselves in order that our triumph can be complete.[3]

Some may repeat the scriptural pleading, "The Lord hath forsaken me, and my Lord hath forgotten me." Or they may need the reassurance from the Lord's promises to us: "But he will show that he hath not . . . yet I will not forget thee. . . . Behold I have engraven thee upon the palms of my hands" (1 Nephi 21:14–16). "I will not fail thee, nor forsake thee" (Joshua 1:5). We have great hope and faith that He will strengthen and enable us in our adversity. After his resurrection He said, "I have drunk out of that bitter cup which the Father hath given me" (3 Nephi 11:11). We too may have to drink from a bitter cup.

How can we endure the bad things that happen to us without allowing them to do bad things to us? How can we keep our faith and find peace and happiness again?

Elder Dennis E. Simmons reminds us,

We must have the same faith as Shadrach, Meshach, and Abed-nego. Our God will deliver us from ridicule and persecution,

but if not. . . . Our God will deliver us from sickness and disease,

but if not. . . . He will deliver us from loneliness, depression, or fear,

but if not. . . . Our God will deliver us from threats, accusations, and insecurity,

but if not. . . . He will deliver us from death or impairment of loved ones,

but if not . . . we will trust in the Lord. Our God will see that we receive justice and fairness, but if not . . . He will make sure that we are loved and recognized,

but if not. . . . We will receive a perfect companion and righteous and obedient children,

but if not . . . we will have faith in the Lord Jesus Christ, knowing that if we do all we can do, we will, in His time and in His way, be delivered and receive all that He has (see D&C 84:35–38).[4]

Notes

1. Theresa Rando (lecture, Association for Death Education and Counseling Conference, Chicago, Mar. 1998).

2. Harold Kushner, *When Bad Things Happen to Good People* (New York: Avon Books, 1981).

3. Neal A. Maxwell, *All These Things Shall Give Thee Experience* (Salt Lake City: Deseret Book, 1979), 43.

4. Dennis E. Simmons, "But If Not . . ." *Ensign*, May 2004, 73.

CHAPTER TWO

Abuse

Many individuals currently living faithful lives suffer with the effects of abuse from their past. Sarah Miller reports that they may even assume that they deserved the abuse, or that somehow it was their fault. Others feel that their abuse is beyond the healing power of the Savior. Church activity can seem overwhelming to these individuals, as they compare themselves with other members and experience feelings of inadequacy. Some ask; "what's wrong with me?" Others wonder why they feel so unworthy if the abuse really was not their fault.[1]

Abuse has many faces and forms: emotional, verbal, physical, spiritual, sexual, and any combinations of the above. Abuse may be intense, violent, and obvious, or begin more subtly and innocently.

Each year in Utah, over 40,000 women (1 in 10) will be subject to physical abuse, and 194,000 to emotional abuse—74.5 percent do not report their abuse.[2]

Emotional and Verbal Abuse

We experience emotional and verbal abuse when someone attempts to control where we go, what we think, who we talk to, or what we say. It is abuse if someone subjects us to any type of physical or social isolation. This type of abuse is often due to extreme jealousy and possessiveness. Perpetrators abuse others by degrading and humiliating them through name calling and put downs. Others exercise unrighteous control or influence by withholding love, communication, and intimacy. There may be false accusation, blame, lying, broken promises, and destroyed trust. We may also receive intimidating looks, gestures, or threats that cause fear, guilt, and shame.

> My parents have threatened to never talk to or support me if I don't do exactly what they want me to do. It is so hard because I love them but I need my autonomy and feel I am only following what God wants me to do.

> It seems the majority of what my spouse says to me is with sarcastic tones, I feel like I am so stupid and of no worth. It really hurts me.

> If I don't do what my wife thinks I should she won't talk to me for hours, withholding any form of love or affection.

Some are able to exercise power over people due to status or money. Men and women experience abuse when their spouses excessively control how monies are spent, restricting access to checkbooks and financial resources including very specific purchases. A woman married to a well-educated and employed college professor reported:

> I was allowed a few dollars per week for my hair to be styled by college students. I was told what food items to buy and how most monies should be spent.

Emotional abuse can evolve into other forms of abuse, including physical abuse.

Physical Abuse

With physical abuse, someone may push, slap, kick, bite, shove, punch, strike, or restrain us. Someone may restrict our sleep, food, water, or medical care. Physical abuse may begin with verbal abuse through threats, criticism, belittling, broken promises, or intimidation.

An estimated 1.9 million women are physically assaulted every year in the United States and over 800,000 men. Most physical abuse occurs at the hand of their intimate partner.[3]

Many women who could and should get out of abusive situations don't. Eleven women in Utah die each year as a result of abuse.[4]

One distraught mother told us:

> I had begged my daughter to get out of her physically abusive relationship. It ultimately cost her life. I am the one who found her a couple of days later in her apartment. I am in total agony recovering from the death of my beautiful young daughter.[5]

"I will not suffer . . . that the cries of the fair daughter . . . shall come up . . . because of the wickedness and abominations of their husbands . . . I will visit them with a sore curse . . . ye have broken the hearts of your tender wives, and lost the confidence of your children" (Jacob 2:31-35).

Child Abuse

Children are often at risk when a spouse is being abused. Of the 4,676 domestic violence cases treated in Utah in 2004, 44 percent were witnessed by children. In some instances, their exposure to violent acts warranted reports to Child Protective Services.[6]

In Utah, 1 in 5 children see or hear verbal abuse, and 1 in 14 will see or hear physical abuse.[7] Utah also reports that 1 in 3 girls and 1 in 5 boys are sexually assaulted before the age of 18.[8]

It is important to inform and educate individuals concerning child abuse. Then it is our duty to protect the child by reporting to Child Protective Services and our bishop when abuse is alleged or suspected. Bishops are counseled to contact the Leaders Abuse Hot Line whenever they suspect that abuse has or may occur to minor children. Reporting abuse is often the only way to hold per-petrators accountable and protect future victims.

"Many men and women have gone out of this life . . . without their vile crimes detected. They may have served in church call-ings; had wonderful reputations, wealth, good health, and glow-ing funeral services. . . . the demands of justice reach beyond the veil."[9]

Sexual Abuse

Sexual abuse is a serious concern in and out of the church. One in five women is sexually abused and usually knows their abuser. Most women never come forward. In Salt Lake City, there were 15,000 reported sexual assaults for 2004. Nationally, in 2006 17.7 million women and 2.8 million men were forced to have sex. Utah's rape rate is approximately 39.1 per 100,000 per year.[10]

Sexual abuse may include forcing sexual acts or behaviors, or hurting a partner during sex. It is also sexual abuse to force a partner to watch sexual acts or to call one's partner by sexually degrading names.[11]

> I grew up with a verbally abusive father. I especially disliked hearing him yell at my mother. I often heard him harshly demanding sex. He was very active in the church and would often apologize in a general way for his bad behavior. After my father's death, my mother would express guilt for some of the relief she felt having him gone. She said she liked living alone

and had no desire to remarry. She seemed happier after his death than she was when he was living.

Unfortunately, sexual abuse occurs too frequently with children. Perpetrators are often someone in a position of power, trust, or control.

The following quote is from a young girl who was sexual abused numerous times in her life:

> Do you think differently of me now? Please don't. I already feel different. Like when my ward went to do baptisms, I did dress out and everything, but when they called me to the font I didn't feel like my body was pure enough to do the baptisms for these people. I felt really bad inside and it hurt to think that my body wasn't clean enough to do it. I stopped saying my prayers for a long time, but just a few days ago I started saying them again and boy did I feel good. I hope I have enough faith in myself that I can do these baptisms.

Then she wrote the following poem:

I said a prayer for you today
And I know God must have heard
I felt the answer in my heart
Although he spoke no word
I asked that He'd be near to you
At the start of each new day
To grant you health and blessings
And a friend to share your way.
I asked for happiness for you

In all things great and small
BUT IT WAS FOR HIS LOVING CARE
I PRAYED FOR MOST OF ALL.[12]

Most young children trust and love their parents unconditionally. They will often deny their own abuse in an attempt to protect and defend their parents or other significant adults. This is one reason why children have a difficult time getting out of abusive situations. Another obvious reason is they are only children with minimal control over their circumstances.

A lamented young man writes:

My father died before I was old enough to confront him with the sexual abuse he had inflicted upon me.[13]

An abused woman said:

It has taken years for me to understand how he could have abused me when I was such a small child. I've finally come to feel sorry for him, let go of the hate, and started to forgive.

A 40-year-old woman revealed that she had experienced sexual abuse as a young girl by her father. He died before she became an adult. In an attempt to help her let go and forgive her father, counseling utilizing visualization and guided imagery was used:

In a safe relaxed state she visualized herself with a large group of people who loved her. The Savior was also present and expressed his love and acceptance of her. When she was ready, she chose to open a door and allow her father into the room. When she first saw her father, she screamed, and verbally confronted him. Through her tears and conversation she realized that he too had been abused and in this safe environment began to feel compassion toward him. She was ultimately able to offer him forgiveness and later claimed her depression had completely lifted.

In contrast to this healing experience, there are situations where abuse victims feel pressured to forgive before they are able. This premature pressure to forgive can produce added guilt. Victims who are already taking too much responsibility for the abuse they suffered now feel additional culpability for not being able to forgive their abuser.[14]

In the April 2008 conference, Elder Scott taught, "When you can forgive the offense, you will be relieved of the pain and heartache that Satan wants in your life . . . if the thought of forgiveness causes you yet more pain, set that step aside until you have more experience with the Savior's healing power in your own life."[15]

A man sexually abused as a child stated:

> I sensed as a young child it was wrong. However, I loved the attention, friendship, and relationship time my abuser offered me. When I became a teenager the sexual gratification became part of it. I knew it was wrong then, it was just hard to break away.[16]

> The sexual abuse of my husband as a young child contributed
> to his homosexuality, which ultimately led to our divorce.

Good people everywhere struggle with the suffering of innocent children. It is difficult to understand why adults would hurt children physically, emotionally, or sexually. God must surely cry with them. The best help for children is often a stable, loving, and supportive parent.

When such a parent is not available or sufficient, professional counseling should be considered.

Spiritual Abuse

Sadly, sexual abuse often leads to spiritual injury. How many prayers will an abused child offer, exercising faith, as he pleads with God to stop the abuse? When the abuse continues, in spite of their faith and prayers, many children experience confusion and begin to question their own personal worth. "Doesn't God love and care about me?" "Isn't this bad enough to warrant God's protection?" "Am I not worthy of an answer to my prayers?" This challenge is further complicated for some when they finally seek help from family or church leaders, only to have their claims denied by the perpetrator and not believed by those whose help and support they desperately need and seek.

> My mother got angry with me when I told her about my
> sexual abuse. She said, "Your brother would never do that!"

Consequently, I couldn't really get the help I needed until I was an adult.

Spiritual abuse may occur when clergy or others in positions of power manipulate or exercise unrighteous dominion over the victim.

> We have learned by sad experience that it is the nature and disposition of almost all men, as soon as they get a little authority, as they suppose, they will immediately begin to exercise "unrighteous dominion" (D&C 121:39).

This form of abuse can cause spiritual injury, confusion concerning deity, and decreased self-worth.

> My church leader told me he was helping me by volunteering to take my sons on outings since I was a single mother. Sadly it turned out he was sexually abusing them.

Some Catholic priests perpetrated spiritual and sexual abuse on their victims. The cost to the Roman Catholic Church has climbed past $1 billion. Over $378 million was incurred in the past several years alone.[17]

The LDS Church and Boy Scouts of America have strict guidelines to avoid such problems. They recommend that men and women working together in callings not travel or spend time paired alone. Church guidelines instruct leaders not to sleep in the same quarters with male or female youth on overnight activities. Spiritual abuse can lead to sexual and emotional abuse.

Getting Help

There is help for the abused and their families. An important principle to remember is that keeping the abuse a secret usually allows the abuse to continue.

> My father sexually abused me as a child. I never sought help because I had heard he went to his Bishop. I assumed he had changed. Many years later he sexually abused my own child. It wasn't until he was finally prosecuted that I found the burden lifted from my shoulders.

"Much abuse involves the denial of feelings and truth, so people who have been abused need to be heard and have their feelings validated . . . Bishops and other supportive members can facilitate healing by empathetically allowing the hurt to find its expression and then offering Christlike love."[18]

Holding perpetrators accountable is important. Pedophiles rarely stop offending unless the abuse is reported and prosecuted. There are therapies and support groups available to help perpetrators change their behavior from the inside out through self-control. Sadly, this change seldom occurs until they have been forced to control their behavior, from the outside in, through close monitoring or incarceration.

Victims of abuse will usually benefit from professional counseling that is consistent with the teachings of the Savior.

You may contact your bishop or LDS Family Services for a referral to a professional counselor in your area. A combination of individual therapy and group therapy is often necessary to ensure successful recovery.

Adults Molested as Children (AMAC) is a valuable resource. AMAC groups offer lessons, discussions, and homework assignments as well as professional guidance and support. Most communities have shelters to temporarily protect women and children who have been or may be subject to abuse, if needed.

There are also sexual addiction support and therapy groups available in the community and through some LDS Family Services offices for sexual perpetrators.

There are often secondary losses and behaviors associated with abuse. The loss of self-esteem, poor body image, eating disorders, sexual problems, nightmares, troubled relationships, excessive need to be in control, addictions, and physical and emotional illness, are all common.

Tools that may be helpful include:

1. Writing a letter to the offender

2. Keeping a journal of feelings and memories

3. Visualizing and confronting the offender (in an empty chair therapy session or through guided imagery)

4. Individual therapy

5. Prayer, blessings, and impressions.

Visions, like impressions, have been a source of knowledge and comfort for many. A stake Relief Society president came to LDS Family Services because she was feeling serious conflict in her life. Initially it seemed that she was simply over-involved in too many worthwhile projects in addition to her own busy calling and family. She gained insight as she identified self-defeating behaviors in her life and was soon able to say "no" without fear of rejection, set some priorities, and cut back.

However, throughout the therapy she didn't feel she was receiving the peace she had desired. One day as she was praying she had a vision. She saw herself as a little girl sitting on a stool in the kitchen with her feet dangling in the air. Her mother was accusing her of not telling the truth. She had just told her mother that her older brother had been sexually abusing her. Her mother told her that her brother would never do that. Her vision of this past painful experience opened up new opportunities to help her. Her recollection was followed by understanding and healing as she was finally able to deal with the true source of her pain and insecurities. Following her insight, she was able to acknowledge the pain, work through the issues, and ultimately let it go and find the peace she was seeking.

We often accept Christ's Atonement for the healing of our sins. Unfortunately, we may not realize His Atonement is infinite and equally able to offer us comfort and healing from our emotional and spiritual wounds. Remember the woman that touched the Saviors garment, hoping for healing from her twelve-year issue of blood. Dr. Terrence C. Smith reminds us that in Jewish law she would have been isolated and cast out, suffering a form of social and emotional abuse for twelve years. Through her faith in God's power she found physical, emotional, and spiritual healing.[19]

The following quote by Elder Vaughn J. Featherstone has provided comfort for the guilt-ridden consciences of many who have suffered as a result of abuse.

> When the future conduct of a violated one is warped and veers away from normal Christian conduct due to early abuse, the Lord will be extremely merciful to those thus forced and violated. It is my belief that the Lord will judge them for what they would have been had the abuse never occurred.[20]

Notes

1. Sarah E. Miller, "Hope and Healing in Recovering from Abuse," *Ensign*, Sept. 2008, 36–37.

2. http:/health.utah.gov/vipp/domesticViolence/overview.html

3. Ibid.

4. Ibid.

5. Joyce and Dennis Ashton, *Jesus Wept* (Springville, Utah: Cedar Fort, Inc., 2001), 47.

6. Utah Division of Child and Family Services, 2004 annual report, 17.

7. Http:/health.utah.gov/vipp/domesticViolence/overview.html

8. Http:/health.utah.gov/vipp/rapesexualassult/overview.html

9. Vaughn J. Featherstone, The Incomparable Christ (Salt Lake City: Deseret Book, 1996), 13.

10. Http:/health.utah.gov/vipp/rapesexualassult/overview.html

11. Http:/health.utah.gov/vipp/domesticViolence/overview.html

12. Ashton, *Jesus Wept*, 49

13. Ibid., p. 50

14. *Ensign*, Sept. 2008, 39.

15. Richard G. Scott, "To Heal the Shattering Consequences of Abuse," *Ensign*, May 2008.

16. Ashton, *Jesus Wept*, 50

17. Ogden Standard-Examiner, 11 Jun. 2005, p. 84.

18. *Ensign*, Sept. 2008, 36–39.

19. Terrence C. Smith, "An Anatomy of Troubles" (lecture, Association of Mormon Counselors and Psychotherapists Conference, Salt Lake City, Utah, Oct. 3, 2008).

20. Featherstone, *The Incomparable Christ*, 12.

CHAPTER THREE

Addictions

Every year, addictions threaten to destroy the lives of over 28 million individuals and their families.[1] Addictions affect our physical bodies, our minds, and spirits. Not only are our jails and prisons overflowing with the devastating consequences of addictive behaviors, but many addicts are Latter-day Saints who are struggling against this powerful serpent. Addicted clientele are the single largest population seeking help from LDS Family Services in the United States.

An addiction is the compulsive use of a substance or activity. The most common addictions are alcohol, drugs, sex, pornography, food, and gambling. Although addictions come in many types and forms, it is not generally helpful to make comparisons promoting one addiction as more damaging than another. The compulsive overeaters claim that alcoholics don't have to drink, but that they have to eat. In reality we all have to eat and drink. Alcoholics must choose to drink other beverages, just as the overeater must abstain from ingesting their trigger foods and bingeing. Some alcoholics rationalize that because alcohol consumption is legal it represents a greater temptation than illicit drugs. However, illicit drugs are small, and easily and quickly ingested, with no noticeable odor like alcohol. Compulsive overeaters may rationalize that food isn't specifically prohibited in the "Word of Wisdom" (D&C 89) like the other addictions, so their addiction is more difficult to overcome.

The sexually addicted have rationalizations and accompanying temptations as well. As computers have contributed the most to pornography addictions, addicts may not even have to leave their home computer in order to view and engage in their addictive behaviors. All rationalizations provide a way of disowning responsibility for one's self-defeating behaviors. The truth is that any addiction can ultimately destroy individuals and family relationships. Even over-doing and abusing good activities including working, exercising, shopping, and church work could cause similar problems. In excess, even "good" activities and behaviors can interfere with personal relationships, spirituality, and family life.

"Satan has a powerful tool to use [even] against good people.

It is distraction. He would have good people fill life with 'good things' so there is no room for the essentials ones."[2]

Serious addictions compromise otherwise capable individuals in their most important roles: 1) home, 2) church, 3) school, and 4) work.

1.   At home, a marriage suffers because trust is violated as the person dealing with an addiction has to hide, deny, and use deceit to preserve his addiction. He is consumed with his own needs (to get a fix) so he is often unable to offer time, interest, intimacy, affection, commitment, and so forth in his responsibilities and relationships. Often his children's everyday needs and demands fall to their non-addicted spouse who becomes over-taxed in her coping abilities. The one suffering from addiction fails to perform and appear at important events, causing feelings of abandonment and resentment from all involved. The associated features are fear, hurt, anger, and loss of communication and security.

2.   At church, the guilt and spiritual injury induced by addictions often cause the one with the addiction to criticize and turn away from his belief system in order to cope and justify his feelings of worthlessness.

3.   At school, addictions not only take time and concentration away from class and studies, but they can cause the brain to become damaged and malfunction. Sleep schedules are altered and attendance and grades soon drop.

4.   At work, people dealing with addictions lose their ability

to interact well with others. They are unable to be dependable or function as productively as in the past.

Over time, addictions may destroy one's physical, emotional, and mental health, as well as spiritual peace.

Alcohol is one of the top health problems in the United States. Latter-day prophets have addressed the problem through the Word of Wisdom (D&C 89), which prohibits the use of alcoholic beverages and other addictive stimulants. Other organizations, including the Catholic Church, have, in their clergy training, focused much attention to the acceptable consumption of alcohol. Learned and sincere men and women have debated for centuries as they have attempted to define what constitutes acceptable "limits" of social drinking, from a spiritual and legal perspective. The following scripture describes well their sincere, yet foolish attempts. "The wisdom of their wise and learned shall perish, and the understanding of their prudent men shall be hid" (2 Nephi 27:26; see also Isaiah 29:14). In contrast, on any given Sunday across the world, Latter-day Saint youth are called upon to share their thoughts and testimonies concerning the Word of Wisdom. They boldly testify in Sunday School, Primary, and in sacrament meetings, that the Lord has asked us not to consume even one alcoholic beverage. Unfortunately, in spite of well-intentioned anti-drug campaigns, religious commitment, and mounting medical evidence, 1 out of 12 Americans becomes an alcoholic.[3]

How Addictions Begin

Addiction often begins when the user experiments with the substance and receives a high or exuberant feeling. Following the first several events, there may be no side effects. The addict thinks it is safe or okay to seek the pleasurable feeling again and again. With time, the user finds he may need more substance to achieve the "high." It may now cost the user more time, energy, and money. Dr. Dean Belnap, MD, often explains that the more the basil ganglion of the brain is stimulated, the more it shuts off the logical decision-making executive center, and spiritual moral conscience of the brain (which is the frontal cortex). Continued misuse of addictive substances can induce similar symptoms and damage as those found in Parkinson's disease.

Due to the stress of addictive habits, the user's family may start to suspect their loved one is using. As time goes on, the user finds that he cannot feel good without the substance. However, his attempts to stop or slow down the addiction repeatedly fail even when he is aware of the consequences. He is robbed of much of his time, which is now spent finding and serving his addictions.

"Thus the devil cheateth their souls, and leadeth them away carefully . . . until he grasps them with his awful chains" (2 Nephi 28:21–22).

The following are segments from the lives of individuals struggling with addictions:

My son has been addicted to drugs and alcohol since he was about 15. It started with alcohol, combined with his low self-esteem and depression. We have tried to get him help many times without much success. He has tried counseling and medication. He struggled to graduate from high school, and has lost many jobs. He has not attended church, nor been morally clean. I worry so much about him. I don't know how to help him. I've cried, prayed, fasted, and put his name on the temple prayer roll. My heart hurts so much as I watch him fail time and time again.

It started at a party. A simple harmless sip. At first I didn't care for the taste, but loved the high that followed. I was freed of my shyness. Everyone laughed at my jokes. My sadness and depression lifted and life looked good. Little did I know that one sip would result in 30 years of alcoholism? It ruined my marriage and I eventually lost my family.

My parents divorced when I was 10. I felt embarrassed around my friends. I found friends that accepted me; however, it meant trying their smokes and drugs. I have been in and out of rehab centers, searching for a way to get out of this trap. I've lost two marriages and countless jobs.

When I discovered that porn was at my fingertips in the privacy of my own home I became addicted. One thing led to another and I lost my church membership and temple marriage.

It started when I got stressed in the mission field. I found that masturbating relaxed me. This eventually led to a pornography internet addiction that almost destroyed my marriage.

We had plenty of money so I felt I could shop whenever and wherever I wished. Soon that was all I was doing. I would leave my children for hours and bring home things we couldn't afford and didn't even need.

I'm not sure what happens to me physically or emotionally. I just start putting food into my mouth and I can't stop. Even when I feel absolutely stuffed I just keep shoving in more food. Sometimes I get so physically sick, I start to throw up. Other times I make myself throw up so I don't get too fat.

After major surgery I was on pain medication for a long time. When I tried to go off of the medication, I got chills, sweats, nausea, insomnia, and an achy feeling all over. When my doctor told me these were withdrawal symptoms from the narcotic, I was shocked. [See the DSM IV p. 141 for more symptoms.] I am still struggling with trying to get off of them. It is frightening to me because my great-aunt had a similar problem which eventually took her life.

There is help and treatment for the addict. Because of the nature of addictions, help ranges from support groups to intensive inpatient recovery programs. There are many addiction recovery programs available in most areas. In 1995, LDS Family Services (LDSFS) began sponsoring support groups under its (ARP) Addiction Recovery Program.

Addiction Recovery Program
LDS Family Services sponsors group recovery meetings to

assist individuals and families who desire to overcome addictive behavior. Through the principles taught in the 12-step program, participants learn that the infinite Atonement of Jesus Christ enables them to overcome addictive behavior.

Recovery meetings are ongoing, confidential, and free. Referrals are not necessary to attend. Experienced group facilitators create a safe environment where participants can share hope, encourage one another, and implement gospel principles in their efforts to recover and heal. A complete list of Addiction Recovery Program meetings is now available on the Church web site.[4]

Because many individuals struggling with addictions to drugs, alcohol, and pornography are unaware of the LDS Family Services addiction recovery program, an effort has been made to inform leaders, members and others of this valuable resource. The following statement may be printed in weekly sacrament meeting programs:

Know someone needing help overcoming an addiction?
Visit http://lds.org. Click on Provident Living, Social Emotional Strength, Addiction Recovery Support Groups, Frequently Asked Questions

If there is not an LDSFS agency in your area, your bishop or branch president may be able to refer you to other community resources. You may also find resources in your area by calling your local hospital or county health department.

The Family of the Addict

Few of us realize how one family member's addictions can affect his entire family. On average, someone struggling with addiction will affect 3 out of 4 family members emotionally, spiritually, or physically. Many family members become hurt, angry, resentful, irritable, and nervous. They often try desperately to change the situation. Codependent family members and others may try to rescue the addict. They attempt to wake them in time for work or other responsibilities. They find themselves making excuses and lying about why he has missed work, stopped paying bills, or has failed to fulfil other commitments. It is not uncommon for family and friends to bail the family member out of jail, perpetuating additional self-defeating behaviors and encouraging deceptions and secrets. Family and concerned friends often pay a heavy price, including their own sanity, in frequent unsuccessful attempts to keep up appearances. It is also not uncommon for families to spend excessive amounts of time and money defending and covering the irresponsible choices and actions of those in their midst who are dealing with addictions.

Due to the denial associated with addictions, recovery often requires confrontation from friends and family members. It takes courage and love to confront the addict with the seriousness of his or her problem. As difficult as it may seem for families and friends, they must generally allow those addicted to experience the consequences of their craving-driven choices. It's very difficult, but important for family members to find ways to show love to the person dealing with addiction, while not facilitating or covering for their addictions and poor choices.

Help for Family

There are support groups and therapies available for family members who may have, over time, become as dysfunctional as the addict. They may need help discovering and accepting that they are not responsible for their loved one's addictions or recovery. They may need help letting go of the guilt, suffering, worry, obsessions, and attempts to control someone else's behaviors. Some need help understanding that they cannot assume responsibility for reforming or changing another person's unhealthy behavior. They need help detaching emotionally, and "letting go, and letting God," They need help realizing that relapses are part of recovery. They need help understanding they are responsible for their own peace, happiness, and recovery. They need help realizing that they are not helping by doing something for others that they can do for themselves. They may need help realizing that they are not helping by covering up. Those who have addictions need help with their distorted thoughts, selfish attitudes, and emotion-driven decision-making.

Al-Anon and other support groups help family members learn about the disease and let them know that they didn't cause the addictions and cannot control the addict or cure their addiction.

Anger, rejection, and silent treatment only add to the guilt and shame that fuels the addiction, especially with those that are active in the LDS church.

Individuals with mental illnesses are more susceptible to addictive behaviors. (See *But if Not . . . Volume II.*)

Tools that help those with addictions accept responsibility:

- Don't attempt to blame, bribe, punish, threaten, or preach.
- Don't play the "poor me" martyr.
- Don't cover for, take over, or hide consequences.
- Don't argue with, destroy substances, or drink with them.
- Do let them know you are studying and learning about their problem.
- Do let them know you are attending support groups for yourself.
- Do accept setbacks and be patient.
- Do spend leisure time together and find new interests.
- Do discuss your situation with someone you trust.
- Do let go of anger, look to your own self-improvement.

Counseling and support groups are available in most areas for family members of those struggling with addictions. Contact your local Bishop or LDSFS. Al-Anon and Alateen are worldwide organizations helping families live with the alcoholic. They discuss the three C's: We did not *cause* our loved ones addictions. We cannot *control* or *cure* those struggling with addictions, only love and support them as they help themselves.

Most addiction recovery support groups follow the Alcoholic Anonymous 12-step support model first introduced in 1935 by Bill Wilson, co-founder of AA and author of the AA Big Book. Recovered addicts believe and profess the following statement:

> I don't think anyone can recover from addictions without sacrifice and complete surrendering by using the principles of the twelve steps.

We will briefly list a modified version of the 12 Steps (the word alcohol has been changed to addiction), with some supporting scriptures.

1. Admit that you, of yourself, are powerless to overcome your addictions and that your life has become unmanageable[5]

> I was in denial thinking I would never do it again . . . over and over . . . until I finally admitted that I couldn't stop the addiction without getting help. The following scriptures confirmed this to me:
>
> I of myself am not more than a mortal man. (Mosiah 2:10)
>
> Oh how great is the nothingness of the children of men (Helaman 12:7)
>
> The greatness of God, and my own nothingness (Mosiah

4:2)

Put on the whole armor of God that ye may be able to stand against the wiles of the devil. For we wrestle not against flesh and blood, but against . . . the rulers of the darkness of this world. . . . Wherefore take unto you the whole armor of God, that ye may be able to withstand in the evil day (Ephesians 6:11-13).

2. Come to believe that the power of God can restore you to complete spiritual health.[6]

Individual willpower, personal determination, motivation, effective planning, and goal setting are necessary but ultimately insufficient to triumphantly complete this mortal journey. Truly we must come to rely upon "the merits, and mercy, and grace of the Holy Messiah (2 Nephi 2:8). . . . Thus the enabling power of the atonement strengthens us to do . . . beyond our . . . natural capacity.[7]

Once I fully realized I could not do it alone I knew I must turn to someone with more power than I possessed.

And my soul hungered; and I kneeled down before my Maker, and I cried unto him in mighty prayer and supplication for mine own soul (Enos 1:4).

Nevertheless they did fast and pray oft, and did wax stronger and stronger in their humility, and firmer and firmer in the faith of Christ . . . even to the purifying and the sanctification of their hearts . . . because of their yielding their hearts to God (Helaman 3:35).

And were it not for the interposition of their all-wise

creator ... they must unavoidably remain in bondage ...
(Mosiah 29:19).

To bind up the brokenhearted, to proclaim liberty to the
captives, and the opening of the prison to them that are bound
(Isaiah 61:1).

3. Decide to turn your will and your life over to the care of God
the Eternal Father and His Son, Jesus Christ.[8]

When we put God first, all other things fall into their proper
place or drop out of our lives.[9]

The great task of life is to learn the will of the Lord and then
do it.[10]

Counsel with the Lord in all thy doings (Alma 37:37).

But if you will turn to the Lord with full purpose of heart,
and put your trust in him . . . He will deliver you out of bondage
(Mosiah 7:3).

Even Christ suffered the will of the Father in all things from
the beginning (3 Nephi 11:11).

Saul (before becoming Paul) when confronted by the Lord
for his sins humbled himself and asked: "What wilt thou have
me do?" (Acts 9:6)

4. Make a searching, fearless, written moral inventory of yourself.[11]

I realized the addiction was only a symptom of my many

problems.

And finally, I cannot tell you all the things whereby ye may commit sin; for there are diver's ways and means, even so many that I cannot number them (Mosiah 4:29).

It may help us to realize that often the root of sin is pride and we may not admit the seriousness of our sins and problems. Alma tells us, "after much tribulation the Lord did hear my cries . . . and has made me an instrument . . . in this I do not glory, for I am unworthy to glory of myself" (Mosiah 23: 10–11).

I, the Lord have suffered the affliction to come upon them, wherewith they have been afflicted, in consequence of their transgressions (D&C 101:2).

And except they repent and turn to the Lord their God, behold, I will deliver them into the hands of their enemies; [addictions] yea, and they shall be brought unto bondage; and they shall be afflicted by the hand of their enemies [addictions] (Mosiah 11:21).

5. Admit to yourself, to your Heavenly Father in the name of Jesus Christ, to proper priesthood authority, and to another person the exact nature of your wrongs.[12]

After I accepted my sin I prayed regularly to God for forgiveness. The hardest part was telling my family and seeing their disappointment and sadness.

And never until I did cry out unto the Lord Jesus Christ

for mercy, did I receive remission from my sins....and did I find peace unto my soul (Alma 38:8).

6. Become entirely ready to have God remove all your character weaknesses.[13]

I wanted to change, I was ready to do it, and I just had to believe that God would help me.

My soul hath been redeemed from the gall of bitterness and the bonds of iniquity. I was in the darkest abyss; but now I behold the marvelous light of God. My soul was racked with eternal torment; but I am snatched, and my soul is pained no more (Mosiah 27:29).

Sanctification cometh because of their yielding their hearts unto God (Helaman 3:35).

Behold, he changed their hearts; yea, he awakened them out of a deep sleep, and they awoke unto God...they were in the midst of darkness; nevertheless, their souls were illuminated by the light (Alma 5:7).

7. Humbly ask Heavenly Father to remove your shortcomings.[14]

I wish I could have the experience of Enos. I am trying to humble myself, "I cried unto him in mighty prayer and supplication for mine own soul . . . and there came a voice unto me, saying: Enos, thy sins are forgiven thee, and thou shalt be blessed" (Enos 1:4–5).

Awake and arouse your faculties even to an experiment on my words. Let this desire work in you (Alma 32:27).

And if men come unto me I will show unto them their weakness . . . for if they humble themselves before me, then will I make weak things become strong unto them (Ether 12:27).

And we talk of Christ; we rejoice in Christ, we preach of Christ . . . that our children might know to what source they may look for a remission of their sins (2 Nephi 25:26).

I was discouraged one night, wondering when I would master this problem; would it ever really be possible? I came upon this scripture following my heartfelt plea to the Lord: "How is it that you have forgotten that the Lord is able to do all things according to his will . . . if they exercise faith in him" (1 Nephi 7:12).

And it shall come to pass in that day that the Lord shall give thee rest, from thy sorrow, and from thy fear, and from the hard bondage wherein thou wast made to serve (2 Nephi 24:3).

8. Make a written list of all persons you have harmed and become willing to make restitution to them.[15]

I have the most wonderful children, I feel so horrible that I have disappointed them and not been there for them. They have all reacted differently to my addiction. Some were shocked, sad, and hurt. Others were furious with me, angry that I have allowed this to be a part of our family.

But if the children shall repent . . . and restore four fold . . . thine indignation shall be turned away (D&C 98:47).

9. Wherever possible, make direct restitution to all persons you have harmed.[16]

I'm not sure how to make it up to my parents; they have been so hurt and disappointed over and over. They have invested time, money and tears.

Ye can do good and be restored unto that which is good (Helaman 14:31).

10. Continue to take personal inventory, and when you are wrong, promptly admit it.[17]

How oft will I gather you as a hen gathereth her chickens under her wings, if ye will repent and return unto me with full purpose of heart. But if not . . . your dwellings shall become desolate (3 Nephi 10: 6–7).

I learned that I may have to deal with cross addictions. Once I abstain from my addiction then other choices sometimes become an issue and I will need to be careful.

And being somewhat of a sober mind, therefore I was visited of the Lord, and tasted and knew of the goodness of Jesus (Mormon 1:15).

11. Seek through prayer and meditation to know the Lord's will and to have the power to carry it out.[18]

It was so disappointing when I would be abstinent for months and then have a slip. The longer my success the deeper the fall and failure seemed. I have, however, learned to get up faster with each fall and turn again to the Lord.

I have had sure answers to my prayers and small miracles in my recovery. The spirit has comforted me.

For I know that the Lord giveth no commandments unto the children of men, save he prepare a way for them that they may accomplish the thing which he commanded them (1 Nephi 3:7).

I try not to forget how great it feels when I pray and feel the Spirit.

Thus we see that the Lord is merciful unto all who call upon his holy name (Helaman 3:27).

The Brother of Jared was chastened for three hours because he remembered not to call upon the Lord (Ether 2:14).

Nothing can make a greater difference in our lives as we come to know and understand our divine relationship with God and His Beloved Son, our Master.[19]

What we really have is a daily reprieve contingent on the maintenance of our spiritual condition.[20]

12. Having had a spiritual awakening as a result of the Atonement of Jesus Christ, share this message with others and practice these principles in all you do.[21]

The healing power of service and lifting others had a profound effect on me.

All these things shall give thee experience (D&C 122:7).

I had learned so much, I wanted to share my hope with others. There are some simple steps that can make a difference.

And the labor which they had to look; and because of the simpleness of the way, or the easiness of it, there were many who perished (1 Nephi 17:51).

God grant me the grace to except with serenity the things that cannot be changed, the courage to change the things which should be changed, and the wisdom to distinguish the one from the other.[22]

May we have the strength, courage, and faith to master our addictions and help others in their recovery.

Thou shalt not be forgotten of me....I have blotted out, as a thick cloud, thy transgressions, and, as a cloud, thy sins: return unto me; for I have redeemed thee (Isaiah 44:21–22).

For more material on addictions see the book: *He did deliver me from Bondage,* by Colleen Harrison Windhaven; and *Hold On to Hope: Help for LDS Addicts and Their Families,* 3rd edition.

We also offer a few more self-help tools and interventions for those struggling with addictions and their family in *But if not . . .*

Volume I.

Notes

1. Mentalhealthlibrary.info/addhelpfamilies

2. Richard G. Scott, "First Things First," *Ensign*, May 2001, 7.

3. http://www.niaaa.nih.gov/FAQs

4. http://lds.org, Provident Living, Social Emotional Strength, Addiction Recovery Groups.

5. *Addiction Recovery Program: A Guide to Addiction Recovery and Healing*, prepared by LDS Family Services, 2005, step 1.

6. Ibid, step 2

7. BYU address, David A. Bednar, "In the strength of the Lord we can do and endure and overcome all things," Oct. 23, 2001.

8. *Addiction Recovery Program*, 2005, step 3.

9. Ezra Taft Benson, "Addiction Recovery Program," *Ensign*, May 1988, 4.

10. Ibid.

11. *Addiction Recovery Program*, 2005, step 4.

12. Ibid., step 5

13. Ibid., step 6

14. Ibid., step 7

15. Ibid., step 8

16. Ibid., step 9

17. Ibid., step 10

18. Ibid., step 11

19. James E. Faust, "That We Might Know Thee," *Ensign*, Jan. 1999, 2.

20. *Big Book of Alcoholics Anonymous*, fourth edition, 2001, 85.

21. *Addiction Recovery Program*, 2005, step 12.

22. Reinhold Niebuhr (http://www.brainyquote.com/quotes/authors/r/reinhold_niebuhr.html).

CHAPTER FOUR

When a Missionary Is Unable to Serve

Many young men and women, as well as their parents, have looked forward to the time when they would become eligible to serve a full-time mission. Most families and church leaders know the benefits of missionary work; not only for the individual lives that are changed as they hear the Gospel, but also for the missionary's growth. We are edified as missionaries return home and share their increased testimonies, recounting wonderful faith-promoting experiences. However, many families are not aware of how difficult or painful the adjustment to the mission field can be. Most young men and women will adjust to their new circumstances and accomplish their goal and dream of bringing many souls into the fold. Unfortunately for others, the dream is shattered as they realize that for a variety of reasons, not every worthy young man or woman will be able to serve a full-time mission.

It is important that individuals, family, and ward members be understanding when a missionary's physical or mental health precludes mission service. Individuals whose desire to serve exceeds their physical and emotional capacity to serve, need and deserve our compassion and support when they must return home early.

President Hinckley said, "Missionary service is extremely demanding and is not suitable for persons whose physical limitations or mental or emotional disability prevent them from serving effectively. . . .Those individuals are honorably excused."[1]

A new elder writes:

> Reality has hit! Not a familiar face in sight. I've had long nights, trying to collect my thoughts and fall asleep on uncomfortable beds with elders snoring. I'm way out of my comfort zone. I feel like I'm losing my personality. I don't feel like the same person at all, like I never existed before the mission.
>
> Love,
> Elder I don't know any more

This loss of self-identity is common to many types of adjustment disorders.

Another elder in the field said:

> My uncomfortable moments still seem to outlast the good ones. I get troubled and hate feeling this way. I'm not sure

what it is that's bothering me [confused by his grief]. I try not to think too much because then I get even more stressed out. [In a noble attempt to focus on missionary work, he denies his grief.] I've developed a lot of ways to deal with things [coping mechanisms]. It's overwhelming.

Recently, a 40-year-old woman told us of her shock when at 21 she arrived in a foreign country to serve her mission. She woke up with flea bites, bleeding through her clothing. She wondered how she could last. She said no one had prepared her for how hard it was going to be. Fortunately she made the transition and loved her mission.

Here are some general qualifications for missionary service that may help us understand why some otherwise worthy members are unable to serve.

1. Physical

Missionaries must be able to work long hours, up to 16 hours a day. They need to be able to walk up to 6 miles a day and ride twice as far on a bike. This routine is physically taxing. A missionary must have healthy eating and sleeping patterns.

2. Emotional and Intellectual

Missionaries should be able to read, learn, and memorize.

A recently called elder with Attention Deficit Disorder writes:

> While reading aloud to my companion through all the rules and things I had to learn in my binder, I stopped as I felt

overwhelmed and tears started hitting the pages. It reminded me of pre-school when I couldn't cut on the lines and tears fell on my work. However, mom came and rescued me then! Mom, where are you now?

Can he or she drive a car and obtain a license? Can she control her emotions? Does he have a temper? Can she interact socially with others? Does he know how to set and accomplish goals? Does he respect authority and follow rules? Can she speak in public settings?

3. Mental

Just as the physical body is subject to illness and malfunction, so is the brain. Serious malfunction of the brain can cause mental illness. (See *But if Not...*, Volume II) Mental illness can cause distortions in thoughts, feelings, and behaviors. Serious mental illness cannot simply be willed away with a positive attitude.

One missionary shares:

> Our family has a history of depression going back several generations. I was confused and frustrated when after several attempts to serve a mission I too, was diagnosed and sent home. It's hard to feel like a failure.

President Hinckley reminds us: "Whatever ailment...a missionary has when he comes into the field only becomes aggravated under the stress of the work... we need missionaries, but they must be capable of doing the work.[2]

Unfortunately, serious struggles and challenges have led, on rare occasions, to a few missionaries tragically ending their own lives.

> My nephew tried to go on a mission two separate times. His depression was so severe he came home from the MTC both times. After he returned for the second time his family found him, dead from a self-inflicted wound.

Individuals with serious mental illness may require professional treatment just as the cancer patient does. Significant mental illness not only affects the missionary, but may also adversely affect his companions and leaders. Missionaries with the following conditions are often not recommended for missionary service: Asperger's disorder, autistic disorder, bipolar disorder (with a history of moderate to severe symptoms) dissociative disorders, eating disorders (moderate to severe symptoms within the past 18 months), mental retardation or borderline IQ (85 or lower), pedophilia (sexual attraction to children), schizophrenia, and other psychotic disorders. Also, extensive use of drugs or alcohol, or individuals with a past history of suicidal ideation or risk may not be recommended to serve. Additionally those needing certain medications such as anti-psychotics may not be recommended to service full time. (For more information see *But if Not* . . . Volume II.)

"Candidates . . .who have had significant emotional [mental] challenges or who are dependent on medication are to have been stabilized [6 months] and found to be fully functional before being recommended."[3]

4. Spiritual

Spiritual preparation is very important for missionary work.

President Hinckley said, "It demands faith, desire, and consecration. It demands clean hands and a pure heart."[4]

Moral worthiness requires that:

> Prospective missionaries who have been guilty of fornication, heavy petting, other sexual perversions, drug abuse, serious violation of civil law and other transgressions are to repent and be free of such for sufficient time (generally not less than one year from the most recent offense). Individuals who have been promiscuous with several partners or who have been with one partner over an extended period of time in either a heterosexual or a homosexual relationship will not be considered for full time missionary service.[5]

Pre-Mission Evaluations

There is a pre-mission evaluation process through LDS Family Services available for missionaries whose psychological health may compromise their ability to serve or whose applications are questionable. LDS Family Services Missionary Clinics provide pre-mission assessments for prospective missionaries. These services (where available) include psychiatric evaluations, medication management, as well as individual and group counseling.

Prospective missionaries may be self- or family-referred. They may also be referred by their church leaders or the missionary department. Pre-mission mental health assessments include professional recommendations regarding the likelihood of the candidate's success as a full-time missionary. Written recommendations are provided to the candidate's stake president and bishop. Decisions concerning a call to serve a full-time mission are prayerfully made by priesthood leaders, after considering the pre-mission assessment recommendations.

Doctors and other professionals in the missionary department also review missionary applications from a medical and mental health perspective. If there is a significant history of mental health issues, the candidate may be referred to an LDS Family Services office or a physician for additional mental and physical health pre-mission assessment.

Early Returning Missionaries

LDS Family Services provides gospel-based counseling, psychiatric evaluations, and educational services for both prospective missionaries and early-released missionaries and their families.

There are also limited counseling services provided by LDS Family Services at the Missionary Training Center (MTC) to help struggling missionaries. Priesthood leaders (following counseling at the MTC or agency pre-mission assessments) will recommend a continuation of missionary service or determine that the missionary should be honorably excused from additional full-time missionary service.

Anxiety is the most common troubling mental health condition seen by LDS Family Services MTC staff. It is commonly manifested as an adjustment disorder, obsessive-compulsive disorder (OCD), or separation anxiety. Other commonly diagnosed conditions include depression, attention deficit hyperactive disorder (ADHD), and learning disabilities.

If a missionary returns home early with serious emotional struggles, LDSFS missionary clinics in Provo, Salt Lake, and Layton provide psychiatrists, professional counselors, and support groups to assist the missionary and his family. Missionary clinics ensure that counseling, medical, and psychiatric services are offered immediately upon the missionary's return home. Separate support groups are offered for parents and the missionary to assist everyone affected by the missionary's un-anticipated early return home from the field.

Services are provided or referral given until stabilization is achieved. If a missionary decides to return to the mission field, he generally must demonstrate stability for six months, and have received a favorable recommendation provided by a professional counselor to his stake president and bishop. LDS Family Services, and other approved professionals can provide these evaluations. Regardless of the counselor's recommendations, final decisions concerning future service are always made by appropriate church leaders after prayerful inspiration.

A follow-up study on missionaries served by the LDS Family Services missionary clinics revealed that 97 percent of the early returned missionaries seen identified themselves as being 100 percent active in the Church two years following treatment.

Preparing Future Missionaries

Brent Scharman lists some basic tools that parents can implement with their children to help them adapt to missionary life.

1. Teach our children to set and accomplish realistic goals and standards.

2. Teach them how to evaluate and solve problems.

3. Teach them to work and manage their time effectively, including getting regular exercise and sleep.

4. Help them to understand the difference between discouragement, everyday ups and downs, and more serious depressions. Excessive worry, guilt, or perfectionism makes it difficult to serve.

5. Teach them basic nutrition facts and not to deal with their emotions through over or under eating or using other substances. Obesity and other eating disorders are very difficult to manage in the field.

6. Teach them about social cues, domestic skills, and money management.

7. Missionaries often struggle with severe homesickness;

prepare children to spend time outside their home by encouraging them to attend Church and scout camps, or go away to school.

8.   Teach them the Gospel, to love the Lord, to serve, feel the Spirit, and to gain a testimony.[6]

After all our love, hard work, faith, and teaching, we then must learn how to accept our own or our children's limitations.

For more coping interventions see *But if not . . .*, Volume I.

Notes

1. Statement on missionary work from the first presidency and the quorum of the twelve apostles, Dec. 11, 2002.

2. Gordon B. Hinckley, "Missionary Service," first worldwide leadership training meeting, Jan. 11 2003, 17–18.

3. Ibid.

4. Ibid.

5. Ibid.

6. S. Brent Scharman , "Preparing your Future Missionary," *Ensign*, Oct. 2004, 17. (Or Dr. Donald Doty, "Missionary Health Preparation," *Ensign*, Mar. 2007, 63.)

CHAPTER FIVE

Coping with and Helping Our Children

Raising children in today's world can be challenging. Parenting is one of the toughest stewardships we may ever face. Most of us have little preparation, and soon learn child-rearing can be difficult even under the most ideal situations. In this chapter we will discuss raising children who are experiencing adversity or dealing with loss and those being raised in blended families after the loss of a parent due to divorce or death.

Rebellious Children

Often, in spite of our efforts to provide a loving gospel-centered family, our children may choose not to follow our teachings and examples.

> Many of our children shall perish in the flesh because of unbelief, nevertheless, God will be merciful . . . and our children shall be restored, that they may come to that which will give them the true knowledge of their Redeemer (2 Nephi 10:2).

A mother writes:

> Why did I think I would escape having rebellious children? Why did I assume I was beyond enduring the heartache I had seen in other parents? Did I assume that I was a better parent? How wrong I was to assume other parents had complete control and could have taught their children better. I had taught my child everything I knew to help her make right choices. We held weekly Family Home Evening. I sent her to good schools where I worked with her teachers. I taught her to be responsible and work hard. I taught her not to steal and return things when she borrows them, she doesn't. I taught her to pay her tithing, she won't. I taught her to live the Word of Wisdom, she doesn't. I taught her to keep a curfew; she won't. I thought I taught her to show respect and obey, but she isn't doing it.

Elder Featherstone suggests that parents who have wayward sons or daughters experience profound and lasting suffering.

He makes the point that losing someone to sin can bring about an eternal loss. In contrast, when we lose a righteous loved one to death, we take comfort in the promise of being reunited with them in the Resurrection if we live worthy:

"Parents of a wayward one have a void and heartache that will not go away until the straying one returns."[1]

The parents of wayward children are often innocent of wrong-doing; however, they suffer deeply watching their child stray.

"If Christ can carry the burden of our transgression, it would only be 'just' that the innocent [parents could] have their pain and afflictions removed."[2]

> I have no greater joy than to hear that my children walk in truth (3 John: 4).

> On my daughter's sixteenth birthday, she asked for leather-bound standard works for her mission preparation class and a CTR ring in gold. She was a 4.0 honor student attending seminary daily. Five months later she ran away from home with a boy in the band at her school. His family hid her for three months until the boy broke up with her. She was sent back to us a different girl. She broke our hearts. She lasted at home for a couple of months. The drugs, alcohol, sex, and party life had changed her. The anti-church environment and anti-Mormon doctrine turned her into a purple, frizzy-haired, modern hippie.[3]

> We suspected our son was involved with alcohol and smoking. We discussed it with him often; however, it didn't seem to make a difference. Eventually it led to worse things. His grades dropped, he lost jobs, and pulled further away from family support. The most difficult event was when he confessed to us he had sex with a girl after drinking. He doesn't care for or even really know this girl!

> Our 19-year-old son has dated the same girl steadily for two years. They are hugging and kissing every day. We have

discussed this close contact with him; however, he doesn't seem to change. We tell him it could lead to an unwed pregnancy. He could lose his opportunity to accomplish his (and our) goal to serve a mission and attend BYU.

Many parents have wondered:

Do we allow her to skip homework, pierce his ear, not pay her tithing, and skip Seminary class, church, or school? Can he date this girl or "hang out" with those guys? How should we discipline curfew violations or too many school tardies? How should we respond to the teen who refuses to do chores, or those who use drugs, cigarettes, or alcohol?[4]

The scriptures provide important insight on the appropriate use of power and influence:

No power of influence can or ought to be maintained by virtue of the priesthood, only by persuasion, by longsuffering, by gentleness and meekness, and by love unfeigned; by kindness and pure knowledge (D&C 121:41–42).

Boyd K. Packer wrote, "The measure of our success as parents . . . will not rest solely on how our children turn out. That judgment would be just only if we could raise our families in a perfectly moral environment, and that now is not possible. It is common for responsible parents to lose one of their children, for a time, to influences over which they have no control."[5]

Elder Packer continued, quoting Elder Orson F. Whitney of

the Quorum of Twelve Apostles, "Though some of the sheep may wander, the eye of the Shepherd is upon them, and sooner or later they will feel the tentacles of divine providence reaching out after them and drawing them back to the fold. . . . Hope on, trust on, till you see the salvation of God."[6]

> For I pray continually for them by day, and my eyes water my pillow by night, because of them; and I cry unto my God in faith, and I know that he will hear my cry (2 Nephi 33:3).

Brother Robert L. Millet teaches, "If our children are sealed to us, we have claim upon the sealing covenant and promise that they will return to us, if not on this earth then in the next. Remember, they were His 'sheep' before they were our children."[7]

Where is My Wandering Boy Tonight?

Where is my wandering boy tonight?
The boy of my tenderest care;
The boy that was once my joy and light,
The child of my love and prayer.
Once, he was pure as the morning dew,
As he knelt at his mother's knee;
No face was so bright, no heart more true,
And none was as sweet as he.
O, could I see him now my boy,
As fair as in olden time,
When cradle and smile made home a joy,
And life was a merry chime.

Go for my wand'ring boy tonight,
Go search for him where you will;
But bring him to me with all his blight,
And tell him I love him still.
Where is my boy tonight?
Where is my boy tonight?
My heart o'erflows, for I love him, he knows,
O, where is my boy tonight?
(Unknown author)

The following scripture reference found in Jacob 5 may apply to the challenge of raising rebellious children; the Servant and Master work long and hard in the vineyard with the tame and wild olive trees:

> What could I have done more . . . should I give up and burn the vineyard? But behold . . . the servant said unto the lord of the vineyard, spare it a little longer (verse 50).

Many members of the Church have had their hearts broken and mourn the loss of their children who choose not to live the commandments. According to scriptural accounts, God lost a third of his children following the war in heaven. We can also read of Enoch's grief and disappointment as he was shown the wickedness of God's children prior to the flood (Moses 7:28, 29, & 37). He cried as he was shown the rebellious children that were drown in the depths of the sea and could not board Noah's Ark (Moses 7:44). However, we can find comfort knowing, "all they that mourn may be sanctified and have eternal life" (Moses 7:45).

It is tragic to see how one child can break the tender hearts of their parents and wreck the spiritual climate in a home. The shattered expectations we have for our children may develop into a significant loss and require grief processing.

We may also be dealing with family traditions and struggles passed on from former generations. Some of the mistakes we make will also be carried into the next generation. An abused child may manifest distrust that contributes to failure in his or her marriage. Children of divorce may be more willing to consider divorce in their own marriages. Generation after generation is perpetuated without a stable, loving, committed, and healthy family. However, it takes just one individual to stop the cycle.

Special needs children (See *But if Not . . .* , Volume II)

> I have an adopted daughter with ADHD [Attention-deficit Hyperactivity Disorder]. No one seems to understand how difficult it is to cope. I feel judged by her behavior; wondering if others think that I'm not a good parent. It is so draining. When my husband comes home at night he says I look so exhausted. I feel others think I am a bad mother because of her behavior. No one seems to understand that we are trying our best to help her. Many members give me advice about how to discipline her, and so forth. Teachers call, frustrated with her in classes at school and church. I didn't know having or adopting children could be so difficult and disappointing. I just don't know if I can cope. I don't see her ever being on her own.

Healthy Families

It is helpful to have a basic idea of what a healthy family is. According to The Family: A Proclamation To The World, families thrive most when parents and children communicate, listen, support, accept, laugh, respect, trust, compliment, play, work, serve, problem solve, pray, and worship together. We are blessed with and accountable to the inspired counsel found in the family proclamation.

It has been said that one of the greatest gifts we can share with our children is a loving marriage relationship. If we are consistent, committed parents, we will have the greatest impact on our children. As soon as our children see we will say "no" ten times, followed by a "yes," they learn to keep asking and we have reinforced their asking up to eleven or twelve times the next time we say "no." We must also agree on discipline and direction (joint front). When one parent gives direction or discipline, the other backs and supports them with consistency and predictability. The exception to this rule would be the responsibility all parents have to interview and protect their children from the abusive behavior of any caregiver including their spouse.

Sometimes it is helpful to ask our children what they need from us during stressful times. A mom and researcher interviewed more than 500 children to learn the kinds of things children consider *least* helpful. Here is what they said:

1.   Indiscriminate praise: Everything I do they tell me is good! Good trying, good finding, good breathing!

2.   Babying: Whenever I go anywhere, they tell me "be careful."

3.   Not listening: My dad doesn't seem to hear what I say.

4.   Not explaining: They say they are going to be consequences but I have no idea what consequences are.

5.   Not showing you care: Telling me all the things I need to do when I get home, instead of asking 'did you have a good day?'

6.   Making idle threats

7.   Public reprimands

8.   Nagging

9.   Blaming

10.   Controlling and ordering, (Afraid I'll mess up).

11.   Bribing. If you want this, you must do that.

12.   Over-scheduling. I can never just hang out.

13.   Misplacement. Ask them to do something and they will say, not now, we are busy.

14.   Negativity (too much criticism).

15.   If I ask why, my mom will say, "Because I said so!"[8]

The following comments are generally road blocks to communication and relationship deflators.

1.   Not now!

2.   You never . . .

3. You always . . .
4. Why can't you be more like . . . ?
5. Here, let me do that.
6. These are the best years of your life.
7. Stop crying. (It can't be that bad.)
8. Stop being so . . .
9. Act your age.
10. You were always such a good boy/girl.

Research indicates that children are most responsive when parents make more deposits of honest praise into their child's emotional bank account and less withdrawals that result from excessive criticism.[9]

It is helpful to understand that each child is born into this world with a different temperament.[10]

We find these temperament differences in a number of areas including:

1. Activity level
2. Emotionality
3. Sociability
4. Self-regulation[11]

"Bring up your children in the love and fear [reverence] of the Lord; study their dispositions and their temperaments, and deal with them accordingly."[12]

Self-Esteem

"It's safe to say that the self image is the core personality ingredient which directs every aspect of our being. The way we communicate, the way we handle our emotions. The way we behave publicly as well as privately is all a commentary on our image of ourselves"[13]

A child's self-esteem and self-worth affects his thoughts and behaviors. Studies have shown that the relationship we have with our children directly affects their self-esteem and confidence. It is important to have a strong spiritual climate and offer a consistent outpouring of daily love shown by physical and verbal affection.[14]

"Those with low self-esteem often perceive a discrepancy between whom they are and who they would like to be."[15]

"Unrealistic expectations can also harm self-esteem."[16]

Everyone desires to be loved and adored. All of us want to hear how wonderful we are and how much we are valued. We can offer this love and acceptance to our families, friends, neighbors, and fellow ward members. We can help others, especially children, focus on the things that they can do rather than the things they can't. This will lift their self-esteem as well as their self-worth. Often we may need to learn to accept, not expect. This does not mean that we don't have rules or discipline for our children. Children with low self-esteem often come from families where there are harsh or over-permissive forms of discipline. Most children respond best to clear, firm, consistent, and loving discipline. Accepting ourselves, our spouse, or our children unconditionally is not always easy. It may mean "letting go" of control. Interdependence is a foundation of self-esteem and may be damaged by attempts to over control individuals. Overly dependent or independent relationship styles are seldom successful in marriage or parenting.

Many children carry negative labels about themselves. They will say things such as "I am ugly," "I am lazy," "I am dumb," "I can't learn," or "No one likes me." These self-defeating statements limit our children's abilities to cope and can damage their self-image. We can help displace these thoughts with new positive labels. Of course parents cannot shield a child from all negative situations. Peers, teachers, and siblings also influence the development of these negative labels. However, "Honest and open communication is the key to preventing self-defeating behaviors from developing and being maintained in our lives."[17]

"Self-defeating behaviors based on faulty perceptions are kept alive and hidden within the individual when either good communication or sufficient love is missing. . . . In those stressful moments, people tend to say or do damaging things to children and let the damaging impressions stand unchallenged and unchanged in the child's mind."[18]

Honest and effective communication is difficult to implement if we are too busy or angry or are grieving. It's during these vulnerable moments that thoughtless or damaging words are often spoken.

"These negative concepts need to be talked out so that the child does not hold them as negative possessions that hinder individuality and limit or cripple potential."[19]

Our son Cameron had cerebral palsy and consequently did not have many of the talents and abilities most children have. We tried to help him feel he was a special child just the way he was. I remember when a little boy asked if he could play with his new Christmas truck and horse. Cameron said, "Yes!" hoping the boy would play with him as well. The young boy picked up the new toy and walked away saying, "No, I don't want to play with you because you're ugly!" Cam responded, "I am not ugly!" (He really was a cute boy, despite his disability.) He handled the situation very well; it was mom who left the room crying! I didn't want Cameron and the others to see my tears and know that my self-esteem wasn't as strong as his! He helped teach our family the true meaning of self-worth and the unique value of each human being.

Dennis would go once a week to Cameron's school and work with Cam and his physical therapist. After several visits he wrote:

> I appreciated the beautiful grin that was always present on Cameron's face when I would walk into his classroom. One week's visit had special significance. Today he was sitting on a small tricycle with his feet strapped to the pedals. He was positioned in the middle of the school hallway. Slowly and with great

effort, he started to move his tricycle toward me! The pleasure, excitement, and pride I felt are hard to describe. Though he had moved only a few inches in my direction, it was the first time in his short life that he had demonstrated his ability to be independently upright and mobile. I realized at that moment that my pride in my son was no less than that of other fathers who had watched their children overcome great challenges and succeed. I knew he would never be the star quarterback for a high school football team, or even compete with his peers in most areas, yet at this moment, I felt joy and pride for a child who was doing his very best with the abilities and talents he possessed.

The things we do, our physical attributes, and the way we dress all have an impact on how we see ourselves on a daily basis and affect our fragile self-esteem. In contrast, self-worth which comes from the inside out, and is based on whom we are, can be permanent. Self-worth is personally controlled internally by those who possess it. Individuals possessing true self-worth are still affected by the loss of friends, possessions, physical health, appearances, [and so forth]. Nonetheless they seem able to find deep within themselves a worth and a value that carries them through difficult times. Unfortunately much of today's values are built upon a self-esteem model that focuses on looks, performance, and obtaining possessions. Our attempt to dress and act in prescribed ways is all designed to increase our esteem and value in society's eyes. Sadly, since the ultimate appraisal of how we are doing comes from others, outside, rather than within, it can be very fleeting. Ultimately our physical talents and possessions will be left behind, and if we do not have internal insight and love of self and others we too may find ourselves lacking the strength to go on in the face of adversity.[20]

Cameron seems to have developed a strong inner strength or self-worth. When asked, "What would you never change about yourself?" He said, "My name." "What is the most important thing you own?" "My wheelchair." "What is your most important achievement?" "To learn to read." "What are you like on the inside?" "Happy." "If your life ended today what would you like people to say about you?" "Hey, that was a neat kid! He also had a cool wheelchair." "Who do you love and admire most?" "God and my mom and dad."

We can hurt a child's self esteem by:

1. Putting them down.
2. Breaking promises.
3. Not allowing them choices and independence.
4. Not giving them respect and privacy.
5. Denying their feelings and personal identity.
6. Not being consistent.

After telling us to love our children, Joseph Fielding Smith counseled: "However wayward they might be . . . when you speak or talk to them, do not do it in anger, do not harshly . . . speak to them kindly . . . you can't drive them; they won't be driven."[21]

The gift of moral agency applies in our parenting and child rearing. Unfortunately, some parents seem to understand the principle of free agency and how to enforce it!

The Lord has asked us to "teach them to understand the doctrine of repentance, faith in Christ the son of the living God, and of baptism and the gift of the Holy Ghost by the laying on of the hands, when eight years old." One of the consequences of not teaching our children is outlined in the Doctrine and Covenants: "the sin be upon the heads of the parents" (D&C 68:25).

How Children Cope with Loss

A child's rebelliousness may be a way of acting out his or her pain and grief. Some may become angry at God or the church because they feel God should have prevented their tragedy or protected them. Spiritual injury may result when a child's prayer isn't answered how they hoped it would be. (See Volume I on "spiritual injury and healing.")

Children can usually sense increased stress and anxiety in their home when parents or siblings are struggling with serious issues. Children should be involved in the open acknowledgement of family issues that directly affect them. Children may experience a loss of trust toward their parents if important issues affecting the family are kept from them. Including children in challenges doesn't mean parents should overwhelm them with their own grief, guilt, sin, and unrealistic expectations. Parents should never involve children in parental conflict that causes them to take sides against any another family member. Parents should never withdraw love and affection as a punishment to one another or their children. Young children cannot fully comprehend a parent's pain. They have developmental limitations for understanding grief, based on their age and limited life experience. Children look to adults, especially their parents, as examples of how to respond to life events. Seeing and sharing our own sadness and disappointments in healthy ways often validates a child's own sadness, confusion, or other emotions. It's a challenging and sobering responsibility to acknowledge that, "parents can complicate or facilitate the grief process for children."[22]

"Children can't tolerate intense emotions for very long. Children generally have a short feeling phase."[23]

Because children may not be developmentally ready to process some aspects of the traumatic event, they often remember and re-grieve certain aspects of their loss as they grow and mature. They may need to relive the experience or grieve at a later time as they mature and grow older. Our 12-year-old son (at the time of Cameron's death) did more of his grief work years later in the mission field when he had the opportunity to work with a young girl dying from a brain tumor.

"Children's emotional symptoms may be slower in surfacing than adults, or even recur later when they reach young adulthood."[24]

We cannot force a child to grieve or react how we would like. We can be available to accept and guide them through whatever phase they are currently in, assisting them when and how they may need us.

"Available evidence suggests that not to assist the bereaved child in actively dealing with the death is to predispose him to significant pathology and lifelong problems."[25]

Children often feel comfort and are reassured when parents make themselves available, share personal testimony, read scriptures, and pray together. Family home evenings can be a forum for family sharing and listening.

Children are often robbed of consistency during tragedies. We shouldn't over-indulge them; however, we should give them our time and love. If left on their own, without support and insight, they may blame themselves or feel responsible for the crisis. In very young children, we may see bed wetting, returning to the bottle, clinging, and phobias.

Encouraging open communication may aid in the healing process. Remember: young children communicate in many ways. Some may communicate subtly and more naturally through their behaviors and play. Others may communicate through art and music. Young boys often grieve through aggressive behavior while many girls become caregivers. Teens may or may not be openly communicative.

A teenage boy wrote after the death of his brother:

> I just wanted to speed my life up about two years and forget what was happening.

We can help children become healthy survivors rather than victims by offering support. We can guide children toward letting go of unrealistic blame and re-channeling their energies into meaningful and productive tasks.

Teens, Trials, and Punishment

Years ago, our 18-year-old son lived away from home for a brief time. One day he called to discuss his new adversities. I realized through this experience how careful we need to be in responding to the misfortunes of children as well as adults. He told me that he had lost his girlfriend and his job all in the same week. As we discussed his sadness, I started asking him if he was paying his tithing, attending church, and reading his scriptures. He said, "Mom, I am not being punished." I thought about his statement off and on over the next several days. I wished I hadn't tried to shame or blame him for his adversity. Then one morning it hit me. My reply to him should have been, "No, you are not being punished; however, if you are keeping the commandments, you are entitled to additional comfort and promptings from the Holy Ghost." God usually will not remove our trials; however, he can comfort us and oftentimes carries us through our most trying circumstances and challenges. His hands, though ever present to sustain and guide us, generally do not take away our trials.

Some children, especially teens, may not want to be involved with the crisis. However, they should still be given the choice.

Children, like adults, fear more bad things may happen. These fears can make them feel vulnerable, fearful, and anxious. Seeing an ill sibling, friend, or relative suffer or receive medical treatments may arouse fears that they might catch the illness or need similar treatments.[26] Children may ask or more likely silently wonder, "What will my future be like?" "Who else will divorce, leave, abuse me, get sick, or die?"

With time, reassurance, and love, a child's security can return. Encourage children to talk and share only if and when they are ready. We shouldn't push or impose feelings or grief upon them that they are not experiencing. We can help them memorialize the ill or dying by allowing and encouraging them to keep something special that reminds them of their loved one. They might benefit from performing a personally meaningful task or ritual. They could play a special game or listen to a favorite song. Some children will enjoy rubbing lotion or oil on their ill loved one's feet or back. Participating in the event is a way of expressing love and concern. Others could help plant a tree or buy a symbolic gift. These activities help children form special relationships with their loved one. The memories of these events can later bring comfort, special memories, and reduced guilt. We should also be prepared for and allow siblings to be children, recognizing their need to play, laugh, and even disagree during adversity. It is not wise to say, "Put it behind you, get over it," or "Be strong, don't cry." These statements encourage children to bury their feelings and promote unhealthy isolated disenfranchised grieving. (See more in volumes I and II.)

Children and Pets

Caring for animals can be a healing tool for children and adults facing adversity and death. A pet can offer unconditional love and acceptance, which may be a source of significant comfort.

Caring for animals also can help children learn that death is part of life. Losing a pet may be a child's first experience with loss.

After Cameron died, we decided to get a dog named Rusty. He was an important part of our family for 14 years, and we all cried and mourned when Rusty died. Adults and children alike can bond tightly with their pets. Remember the song "Mr. Boe Jangle"? Boe and his dog traveled and performed together for many years. A strong bond was formed between man and dog as they worked side by side. When his dog died, Boe was lost for a time. He had lost his best friend as well as his employment. Unfortunately his grief turned to depression. He turned to alcohol in an attempt to numb his pain and spent time in jail.

We should resist the impulse to immediately replace our child's lost pet. We should provide them with the time and opportunity to cry and mourn. We can also help them bury their pet. We can allow them to decide if and when they desire another pet. Avoid the temptation to run and buy another pet in an attempt to negate the loss and stop your child from grieving.

Children and Funerals

Children are exposed to 8,000 murders and more than 100,000

other acts of violence on TV by the time they leave elementary school.[27] They are rarely shown the aftermath of grief that inevitably follows death. Few are prepared to deal with the realities and consequences of a significant personal loss.

A funeral may help children actualize the event and their loss. Most children can and should be invited to attend a loved one's funeral. If they are old enough to love, they are generally old enough to grieve and participate. It is appropriate to ask them if they'd like to go to the funeral. Explain what will take place, and what they will see. They could also participate in the program if they so desire. For example, they could write a letter or a song to the deceased that could be shared, if appropriate. Dennis and I left our 4-year-old home during his grandfather's funeral. When he was 15 years old he told us he wished we had let him go. We took our almost 3-year-old daughter to her brother's viewing and funeral. When she saw her brother in the casket she said, "That's not Cameron." She was visibly upset and pushed to get away! We asked a friend to sit with her in the back of the chapel during the funeral, because she wouldn't sit still. Later, she didn't want to look at the pictures of her deceased brother in the coffin, the very same pictures that brought us comfort. Fortunately, years later, she remembers none of the negative events and seems focused on her pleasant memories of Cameron. She also chose later to view his pictures.

The function of funerals or other death rituals is:

1. To acknowledge death and accept our new reality.
2. To remember and recall.
3. To receive support.
4. To express love and encourage emotional release.

Teaching Children About an Afterlife

Studies show most bereaved parents believe in life after death. They hope for a reunion with their child.[28] The following analogy may help parents verbally convey their belief and hope in an afterlife to young children:

> Have you ever seen a butterfly? Did you know it was a caterpillar first? [Explain the cocoon and its process.] Your brother's body lying so still [use the words dead, dying, die, not asleep] is the shell he left behind, like the cocoon when the butterfly leaves. His spirit or soul has gone or flown to another place, [heaven] just like the butterfly flies away.

Another visual aid helpful for young children requires your hand and a glove:

> This glove represents or is like your brother's body lying here so still in the casket. [Take your hand out of the glove and lay it down.] The glove, like your bother's body is now empty. [Move your hand toward the sky.] Your brother's spirit, represented by my hand, has gone on to another place we call heaven.

Blended Families

A blended family occurs when two people, each with children

of their own, decide to marry and form a new family union. This usually occurs due to death or divorce.

Blending families can be a challenge. Knowledge and understanding of the process and what to expect can help. There are also many interventions that can help make the process more successful.

It is important to realize that children may be still grieving the loss of their former parent when the new marriage takes place. There may be fantasies that mom and dad will reconcile some day. Some children fear that their parent will love the new siblings more than their own biological children. This can bring waves of hurt and anger for children.

With the death of a parent, a new marriage may bring sadness and grief, a reminder of what has been lost. All of these changes and emotions may make it difficult to blend families; however it can be successfully accomplished.

It would be helpful for parents to learn and acquire education and information about blending and step parenting. Some information that Brent and Jan Scharman share may be helpful:

1.   Realize that any major change or loss in life often takes years to adjust and adapt.

2.   Professionals recommend that the biological parent do the disciplining of their own children whenever possible.

3.   Both parents should keep some of the old traditions while planning and experiencing new ones.

4.   Exercise flexibility with your rules and try to give each child his own space and privacy.

It is possible to successfully blend families and have love and joy again in family life.[29]

Notes

1.   Vaughn J. Featherstone, *The Incomparable Christ* (Salt Lake City: Deseret Book, 1996), 9.

2.   Ibid, 10.

3.   Joyce and Dennis Ashton, *Jesus Wept* (Springville: Cedar Fort, Inc., 2001), 41.

4.   Ibid, 220.

5.   Boyd K. Packer, "Our Moral Environment," *Ensign*, May 1992, 66.

6.   Ibid.

7.   Robert L. Millet, *When a Child Wanders* (Salt Lake City: Deseret Book, 1996).

8.   The Parent Institute, *Parents Make a Difference* [newsletter, 1993].

9.   F. Covey, "Strengthening the Family" (lecture, Association of Mormon Counselors and Psychotherapists Conference, Salt Lake City, Utah, Apr. 1999).

10. M. K. Rothbart and J. E. Bates, "Temperament," in *Handbook of Child Psychology*, 5th ed. (New York: Wiley, 1998), 105–176.

11. T. D. Wachs (1999), "The what, why, and how of temperament: A piece of the Action," in *Child Psychology: A Handbook of Contemporary Issues* (Philadelphia: Psychology Press, 1999), 23–44.

12. John A. Widtsoe, comp., Discourses of Brigham Young (Salt Lake City:Deseret Book, 1978), 207.

13. Dr. Les Carter, "Self-Esteem" (radio talk show), Minirth-Meier Media Ministries, Jun. 15, 1994.

14. Brent L. Top and Bruce A. Chadwick, "Helping Children Develop Feelings of Self-Worth," *Ensign*, Feb. 2006, 33–37.

15. Dunn and Hargett Inc., *Growing Together* [Newletter, 1993], No. 2, Vol. 9-3.

16. The Parent Institute, *Parents Make a Difference* [Newsletter, 1993], No. 4, Vol. 4-4.

17. J. Chamberlain, *Eliminate Your SDB's* (Self-Defeating Behaviors), (Provo: BYU Press, 1978), 161.

18. Ibid., 162

19. Ibid., 162

20. J. Ashton & D. Ashton, *Loss and Grief Recovery* (Amityville: Baywood Publishing, 1996), 52–3.

21. Joseph F. Smith, *Gospel Doctrine*, 5th ed. (Salt Lake City: Deseret Book 1939), 316.

22. K. Doka, "Living with Grief" (lecture, Hospice Foundation of America National Teleconference, VA, Apr. 4, 1999).

23. A. Wolfelt, "Grief" (lecture, Association for Death Education and Counseling Conference, Chicago, IL, Mar. 1998).

24. Ashton, *Loss and Grief Recovery*, 118.

25. T. A, Rando, *Grief, Dying and Death* (Champaign: Research Press, 1984), 155.

26. S. M. Thibodeau, "Sibling Response to Chronic Illness: The Role of the Clinical Nurse Specialist," *Issues in Comprehensive Nursing*, no. 11 (1988): 17–28.

27. Children Television and Violence, Abelard.org/tv/tv.php, 1998.

28. Knapp, R. J., *Beyond Endurance—When a Child Dies* (New York: Schocken Books, 1986), 35.; Doka, K.J. &J.D. Morgan (Eds.), *Death and Spirituality* (Amityville: Baywood Publishing, 1993), 65.

29. Janet Scharman, "Blended Families" (lecture, Families Under Fire, Provo, Utah, Oct. 3, 2005).

CHAPTER SIX

Divorce

Divorce is the legal ending of a marriage. No one marries and then plans for divorce. The death of a marriage is painful, lonely, and complex, and may follow many years of painful marital discord. There are no funeral services, sympathy cards, condolence calls, or flowers sent. Divorce can affect one's personality, role, and identity in dramatic and damaging ways.[1]

Divorce is especially devastating if you've grown up in the church believing that someday, if you're worthy, you can be married "forever" in a temple of God. Establishing an eternal family is the hope and dream of many wonderful LDS couples. Fortunately, we do have many wonderful marriages and families in the church where everyone works together to realize these promises.

Unfortunately, there are far too many others whose dreams are shattered in spite of their wholehearted and righteous efforts.

A divorced mother said:

> All my hopes, dreams, prayers, and energy have gone into my temple marriage. I am still in shock that it is gone. How did this happen?

Why Do Couples Divorce?

A 1994 marriage and family study lists, in order, the most common reasons couples divorce:

1. Infidelity
2. No longer in love
3. Emotional problems
4. Financial problems
5. Sexual problems
6. Problems with in-laws
7. Neglect of children
8. Physical abuse
9. Alcohol
10. Job conflicts
11. Communication problems
12. Married too young[2]

When Is Divorce Justified?

Ending a marriage is usually a heart-wrenching decision. For most Latter-day Saint couples, to let go requires much prayer, fasting, and revelation. Each couple's circumstances are different and ultimately they are responsible to determine their own outcomes. However, married couples who struggle with chronic addictions, substance abuse, psychosis, extreme mental illness, and physical or mental abuse have marriages that often end in divorce.[3]

Infidelity is listed as one of the top twelve reasons couples divorce. The truth is that many marriages can survive a sexual indiscretion; this occurs when the offended partner is willing and able to work through the initially overwhelming disappointment and loss of trust. Mira Kirshenbaum, PhD discovered that couples are able to forgive the first affair when *both* are willing to try to build trust again; however, if an affair occurs a second time, the likelihood for a successful marriage is seriously compromised.[4]

President Faust said of divorce, "In my opinion, 'just cause' should be nothing less serious than a prolonged and apparently irredeemable relationship which is destructive of a person's dignity as a human being."[5]

A divorce usually brings about a division of debts, assets, and property. It may also include the payment of spouse and child support and the assigning of parental rights.

We have watched close friends and relatives, as well as clients endure divorce. Some individuals view their divorce as an *eternal loss* because of the catastrophic consequences that they feel extend beyond earth life. Friends and family often offer comfort to those who have lost a loved one to death by reassuring them that they will eventually see and hold their deceased loved one again in the eternities. It is often much more difficult to comfort men and women who have lost an eternal mate to divorce.

A recently divorced member said:

> I grew up in the church, married a returned missionary in the temple after fasting and praying to confirm my decision. My husband and I have always been worthy and active in the church. Last year my husband told me he didn't love me anymore and wanted a separation and probably a divorce. I was overcome with shock and confusion. How could this happen? I feel so helpless and hopeless. I have prayed, fasted, and attended the temple begging for God's help. I pray that my husband will return, or that I can find some permanent peace and resolution. Neither has occurred yet. I feel I am worthy and have faith for a miracle. I have done everything possible to ensure a good life and a temple marriage. I don't feel as comfortable at church. I feel everyone is looking at me, feeling sorry for me, or wondering what I did to drive my husband away. The sacrament talks and lessons in Relief Society don't offer much comfort right now. My husband has told me he cannot afford to pay for two places to live, so I must look for work. I'm not sure I am capable of so much stress right now. What will my children do? How will they cope with their father leaving, and now me going to work? What has happened to my eternal family? It's hard to want to go on when the most important thing to me is gone.

We believe God is just and will, over time, compensate for the pain parents and children experience because of divorce. Until then, how can we support those in the church who have experienced what many consider an eternal loss?

Even when couples consider divorce, it is common for one spouse to continue fighting for his or her temple marriage.

During and following a divorce it may be difficult for some grieving family members to attend church meetings. The following is a journal entry of a divorced member:

> Today it was hard to be at church. They showed part of a video called "Families are Forever." It's awful for a divorced person to realize that we no longer have a complete family. I feel it sometimes pulls people away from the church . . . I need to remember to follow Christ and believe Christ. He has promised that if I do what is right I will have all that he has. That means a "forever family."
>
> (Later) When I look through my journal now, it upsets me. I see how I was so consumed with justification that I couldn't enjoy life. . . . I was trying to do my best and I didn't feel it was good enough. My spouse said that one of the reasons he left was because I made him feel guilty. I told him I didn't mean to "guilt" him and that I would go to counseling and learn how to improve communication. "No," his mind was made up. This made me carry more guilt. One thing I would say to a person going through divorce, "Get rid of guilt, it doesn't do any good. Guilt gets you nowhere."[6]

Part of the guilt she was suffering from was "false guilt"—feeling guilty for events that were outside of her personal agency and control. In contrast, true guilt for willful wrong doing will lead us to repentance and personal growth as we change our own sinful behavior.

> I called my sister today. She is in the depths of despair. She just finished her first week of full-time employment since her husband left about a month ago. She was physically and emotionally exhausted, and so sad. It was Easter Sunday and she had watched General Conference and tried to find comfort in the Atonement and the words spoken. She desperately wants to keep her husband, temple marriage, and children together. She asked me why Alma's father's prayer was answered by an Angel appearing and convincing his sons and Mosiah's sons to repent. Why didn't the same angel convince her husband to repent and stay with his family? She asks, "Why do some people receive a miracle, while others do not?" She is a worthy member, with faith as strong as any I've known. She was so sad and depressed. She thought of asking her kindergartner to come and kneel by her bed and pray for her as she lay sobbing. She wondered if maybe the faith of a child's prayer would relieve her agony. I thought of the Savior who felt the pain of the world's sins in Gethsemane. Please let this cup pass. She also said she was hoping for a car accident to remove this pain and the future without her eternal companion. I cried with her, realizing her pain was beyond my comprehension. Will a new mate be provided? When and how? Could she and the kids love him as much as their biological father? So much faith is required.[7]

A child writes about her plea to God:

> I remember getting down on my knees and asking my Father in Heaven to please help my parents to not get a divorce. When

I received no answer, I felt all alone, like I wasn't getting any help for the pain I felt. It hurt for a very long time. I don't think I ever got over not getting my answer. [see "Spiritual Injury" in Volume I] With time I accepted that my parents were going to get a divorce."

A teen writes:

My dad was excommunicated before my parents' divorce. It was embarrassing to have friends over, so I didn't do that much. My mom showed her anger even in front of my friends. I turned to my peers, especially boyfriends.

I received some spiritual impressions and insight today. I was doing the laundry, of all things. I was feeling confused about life and God's intervention in it. I had just talked to several women whose husbands had left them and their families. As I listened to their pain, I wondered how God could stand to watch their suffering and not cause a great miracle and take away all of the pain. Why didn't he intervene and change their situations? The words that came to me were simple. I had heard them a hundred times before. But now the power of the spirit overwhelmed me. What I heard in my heart was this: "The Lord, God, knows the end from the beginning." (Isaiah. 46:10; 1 Nephi 9:6)

Robert L. Millet comes to a similar revelation as he shares the time he was struggling with "wandering souls" in his family. A caring colleague asked him if he thought Heavenly Father moped around the heavens over his straying children. After he said no, he concluded that the reason was God, "[knows] the end from the beginning," or His eternal perspective.

As we remain faithful and endure to the end, we too may find comfort in this same eternal perspective.

The divorce rate in the United States is about 50 percent.[8] Many divorced individuals choose to stay single while others decide to give marriage another try. (See chapter 9, "Never Married.")

Marrying Again

Many divorced individuals wonder if they could, or should, marry again. Of course this is a very individual decision with varied answers and circumstances. Children may still be grieving the loss of their former parent when the new marriage occurs. With divorce, children may fantasize that mom and dad will reconcile some day; thus, a new marriage can bring waves of hurt and anger. With death, a new marriage may be seen as a betrayal of love and memories. Blending families with all of these emotions will be difficult, but can be successfully accomplished.

Marriages often fail as a result of the stress experienced from a significant loss. The loss of a child, for instance, too often results in a secondary loss of the marriage. The accumulative grief resulting from such multiple losses can be devastating to families; however, if we allow all family members to fully mourn and deal with their grief, they can usually love and live well again.

"They shall obtain gladness and joy; sorrow and mourning

shall flee away. I am he; yea, I am he that comforteth you" (2 Nephi 8:11–12).

Notes

1. Association for Death Education and Counseling, *The Forum* [Newsletter, 1998], May/Jun.

2. David H. Olsen, and John Defrain, *Marriage and the Family, Diversity and Strengths* (Mountain View: Mayfield Publishing, 1994), 552.

3. Diane Medved, *The Case Against Divorce: Discover the Lures, and the Emotional Traps of Divorce—Plus the Seven Vital Reasons to Stay Together* (New York: Donald I. Fine, Inc., 1989), 121.

4. Sara Eckel (quoting author Mira Kirshenbaum, PhD), *The Lowdown on Cheating* (AOL Women's Channel), http://relationships.blogcity.com/lowdown_on_cheating_1.htm (accessed Jun. 28, 2008).

5. James E. Faust, "Fathers, Mothers, Marriage," *Ensign*, Aug. 2004, 3.

6. Joyce and Dennis Ashton, *Jesus Wept* (Springville, Utah: Cedar Fort, Inc., 2001), 38–9.

7. Ibid., 39–40.

8. Terrence C. Smith, "An Anatomy of Troubles" (lecture, Association of Mormon Counselors and Psychotherapists Conference, Salt Lake City, Utah, Oct. 3, 2008).

CHAPTER SEVEN

Help for Marriage During Unexpected Loss

Good marriages don't just happen. Marriage is an ever-changing and demanding venture requiring constant attention. It will require extra time, patience, and love when your marriage is experiencing an unexpected crisis. Every marriage has degrees of conflict woven around love and joy. It is when needs are not met and the conflict cannot be resolved that marital discord becomes a problem. It takes hard work, flexibility, responsiveness, sensitivity, compromise, tolerance, and forgiveness to make a marriage work under any circumstances.

Many scholars believe that 50 percent of the marriages in the United States end in divorce.[1] Divorce is less likely for those in the United States who marry in a church. In contrast, the lifetime divorce rate for temple marriages is estimated to be no greater than 20 percent.[2] Church members who marry in the temple are five times less likely to divorce than church members who have a non-temple marriage.[3]

There are gospel principles, many of which are listed in The Family Proclamation, that provide support and direction to our marriages. We will discuss specific marriage practices that can contribute to successful matrimony as couples endure loss.

Common Stressors

As stated in the previous chapter on divorce, the most common reasons couples list for giving up on their marriages are: 1) infidelity, 2) no longer in love, 3) emotional problems, 4) financial problems, 5) sexual problems, 6) problems with in-laws, 7) neglect of children, 8) physical abuse, 9) alcohol, 10) job conflicts, 11) communication problems, and 12) married too young.[4]

Another common stress among church members occurs when one spouse is not as active or committed to the gospel or their temple marriage as the other. Conflicts develop as couples attempt to adapt to each other's varied differences, including spiritual issues. Differences that seem to threaten the eternal covenants are often the most painful to accept. One may feel cheated or robbed from a more ideal partnership that was imagined, expected, or even promised during the courtship, temple sealing, or early years of marriage. These lost dreams and expectations can lead to resentment and bitterness between couples. As a result the other spouse often feels judged, unloved, or condemned as not being "perfect" or "good enough."

> I have thought of divorce off and on for years; the biggest reason is the lack of spirituality in our marriage. I finally thought our spiritual life was on its way because my husband of fifteen years decided he would give up his vices and take me and our children to the temple. I was thrilled! However, my excitement didn't last long. A few months after our sealing, we bought a computer and my husband started spending time on the Internet. He has gotten into sexual conversations and pornography. I feel afraid. He has also stopped our scripture reading together and he doesn't read alone. He doesn't have much desire to attend church or the temple. I also feel trapped because getting a divorce would be more difficult now because we have a temple marriage. Does God expect me to love and accept this man when he is not living the gospel?

Expectations of how one's spouse will abide by the laws and commandments are often formed from childhood. An active Latter-day Saint wife shared the following concerning her marriage to a non-member:

> I joined the church after I was married. My husband has allowed me to practice most of my new LDS religion for 30 years now. I cannot pay tithing on his money, just on mine. He provided for our son to serve a mission and our daughter to be married in the temple. He doesn't want me to go to the temple because he doesn't want me to wear garments. He drinks;

however, he doesn't pressure me to. He allows us to attend church on Sunday; however, afterwards he expects us to do what he wants to do or go where he wants to go. It is very hard. I have thought of divorce off and on over the years, but have chosen to stay, hoping someday he'll convert.

Marital discord may also be a result of a couple enduring difficult life challenges and loss. They may experience grief and pain as they struggle to keep their marriage intact.

A grief-stricken father stated after losing a child:

> My wife is not the same person that I married and neither am I. We are suffering so many losses.

At times bereaved parents experience grief that is so intense that their "physical or emotional symptoms and defenses block the growth in the relationship."[5]

Basic Human Needs

Humans need water, food, shelter, and love to survive. It is helpful to understand some of the basic needs of individuals in a marriage relationship as well:

1. Affection and touch
2. Acceptance and belonging
3. Communication
4. Friendship, freedom, and fun together
5. Security and trust

6. Sexuality
7. Spirituality

For varied reasons, couples may not be able to provide these essential needs for each other. In fact, when men and women are asked to prioritize their needs in order of importance, we often find striking differences. A common difference is that men list the importance of sex higher than women do; while women list the importance of communication and understanding of their feelings higher than men do. It is helpful for couples to realize how contrasting their preferences can be. Some call this "learning your mate's love language." For example, I promise Dennis a long back rug (touch and affection are his love language) if he will do chores around the house for me. (My primary love language is tasks.) Dr. Willard F. Harley's research revealed that men listed the following in order of preference from their wives:

1. Sexual Fulfillment
2. Recreation Companionship
3. An Attractive Spouse
4. Domestic Support
5. Admiration

Women listed the following preferences in order from their husbands:

1. Affection
2. Conversation

3. Honesty and Openness
4. Financial Security
5. Family Commitment[6]

Difference in Men and Women

We are very aware of men's and women's biological differences. In addition, young girls are often raised with different expectations than boys are raised with. For instance, boys are generally encouraged to be strong and silent, while girls are encouraged to express their emotions. Society encourages numerous divergent roles for men and women that become blended with cultural and other stereotypes. The following four P's elaborate on some of these differences.

The Four P's

1. **PROTECTORS**: Men learn early that their primary role in society is to protect their family and property from harm. A bereaved father said: "When our daughter died, I felt as if I had failed to protect her. I think there were things I could have done to prevent what happened." Men also feel a specific responsibility as patriarchs in their homes. When challenges occur, men often feel a sense of failure. He may have prayed, fasted, and offered blessings that didn't seem to help. Watching his wife or family suffer due to a major challenge constitutes an additional secondary loss for men. If women are single, they may assume the protector role

for their children.

2. **Providers**: Most men feel more responsible for the finances than women do. It is often the man who returns immediately to work after a challenge or tragedy. The woman may spend more time at home in nurturing activities for her and her children. A man may push his worries aside by working the long hours he perceives are needed to more adequately support his family. He may also use his work to escape his painful realities. One woman's reaction to tragedy was evidenced by her response to her husband's attempt to cope with his own pain:

> I couldn't understand how he could just go right back to work after our tragedy. I would lie awake at night worrying and listening to his peaceful snore.

3. **Program Controllers**: Both men and women like control. However, men generally cannot handle feeling helpless or out of control as well as women do. Often when tragedy comes, so does the fear of losing control over their stewardship. Their assumptive world has been assaulted.[7]

One widower writes of his helplessness:

> The loss of control in my life is, at times, as overwhelming as my spouse's death.

Women frequently report feeling overwhelmed when confronted with the realization that there is not enough time to do all that they want to do and or feel is required of them.

4. **PROBLEM SOLVERS**: Men are often programmed more than women to "fix" everything. They feel responsible to find a cure or solution. When men or women learn they cannot fix or change their circumstances, they may feel a sense of failure and guilt. Men seem to struggle more than women do when they feel powerless. One man writes after the drug-induced death of his son:

> I was so mad at our son for putting us in this position. I also felt guilt at not being able to help him with his problems.

It may be helpful for couples to realize that differences between men and women are common and should be expected and accepted. It will take time, energy, tolerance, and healthy thought processes to work through each couple's unique issues. It may also be helpful to remember that husbands and wives each have unique and changing needs relative to closeness and separateness. Problems may occur when one person's need for closeness threatens the other person's need for separateness.

In addition to men and women's bodies being biologically different, there also seems to be a difference in how men's and women's brains function. These functional differences can affect thoughts, moods, and behaviors. Additionally, men and women have different hormones that influence feelings and behaviors.

Men and women may evaluate their lives from different paradigms as well. Women generally see their lives as a "whole." If something goes wrong, such as a small flaw in her life, personality, or behavior, they often judge themselves (or their whole life) harshly. This is sometimes called, "all or nothing thinking." An example might be a sister teaching a Relief Society lesson. She has worked on her lesson for weeks, has beautiful visual aids, handouts, and so forth. However, when the special recorded music fails to function properly, she leaves discouraged, thinking her whole lesson was ruined. If you go down the hall the same Sunday to the High Priest Quorum, you might find that a quorum instructor has forgotten altogether that it was his turn to teach the lesson. He calmly asks if someone brought their manual which he quickly borrows as he and the other brethren begin to discuss the lesson. He and most of the other men go home thinking the class went well while debating and kidding about who will win the next big game!

Men often view, evaluate, and segregate their conflicting thoughts and behaviors individually into independent compartments within their consciousness. For example, a man can be a wonderful father and church leader and still not feel guilt from speeding on the highways, or cussing and losing his temper during a church basketball game. The predisposition of not focusing on conflicting behaviors diminishes his feelings of guilt. Men are usually able to positively view their overall life and self, even when they struggle and fall short in certain areas. On the other hand, women seem to focus more on their weaknesses and are not as likely to rationalize or ignore their faults as easily as men. When you add all these differences to other variables such as family background, coping style, personality, past modeling, beliefs, and values, you can see why a husband and wife may react differently over the same experience or difficulty. A mother raising a disabled teenager now fearing she's pregnant with a Down's syndrome baby writes to her deceased two year old daughter:

> I think I would be able to handle things a lot better if I knew this baby was okay. *Is it okay?* I keep thinking over and over of the night you died. It breaks my heart! Am I missing something, am I forgetting something, did I do something wrong to make you die, to leave us? Why did we lose you? You were the best thing to happen to our family. The other two kids have had a lot of problems lately. What is to become of us? Can we ever feel peace and joy in this life ever again? It is so hard for me to talk to people in the ward about my troubles. They don't understand. *Even daddy doesn't understand how I feel*! I love you. Mom.[8]

With time this mother was able to understand and accept that others, including her husband, grieve in different ways.

Prophets have spoken on the different roles of men and women in a harmonious marriage. For further reading on this subject, review The Family: A Proclamation To The World.

Self-help Tools

What we like to refer to as the "Four Marital C's" can significantly influence and strengthen marriage relationships during difficult times including unexpected loss and stress:

1. Commitment
2. Communication
3. Cooperation and Tolerance
4. Conflict Resolution

1. **Commitment**: Being committed to each other and to the marriage is a powerful ingredient found in marriages that endure serious life challenges. Those who do not consider divorce as an option, before they exhaust all other possibilities, are more likely to find mutually acceptable solutions that help keep their marriages intact.

2. **Communication**: Lack of communication often contributes to a couple's decision to divorce. One partner may blame, the other then isolates or withdraws from the relationship. The absence of disclosing and responsive interactions can begin the process of relationship distress. When couples are exhausted, stressed, or mourning, it is difficult to find the time and energy vital for interaction. Remaining open and honest, and frequently discussing trials and challenges will enhance meaningful communication.

It's important for men to remember that most women process their thoughts, concerns, and decisions verbally. They think aloud and may say things they are only considering and espouse solutions when they are actually questioning. Women (especially prior to their menses) are usually more expressive of their emotions than men are. Women will do well to understand that men often process thoughts and ideas silently. It may take a man several minutes, an hour, or longer before he is able to reveal his innermost feelings in verbal answers to his wife's questions.

It is estimated that men speak about one third as many words per day as women. Men often use up their comfort level of words at work, which explains their silence at home. Mothers and homemakers who spend their days with children may have most of their words left in reserve waiting to be expressed in adult conversation with their husbands at the end of the day. Too often when her husband finally arrives home, tired from all his work and adult conversation, he is ready for peace and quiet.[9] If a husband can listen and validate his wife's feelings, and if a wife can avoid pressuring her husband to speak or answer all her questions immediately, their relationship will develop more smoothly.

Allowing for the expression of negative and ambivalent feelings can be healing. It is hard for some individuals to accept and share their feelings because they fear being judged or labeled. Acknowledging and validating feelings and opinions is more valuable than attempting to judge those feelings and opinions as being right or wrong. One's feelings are usually present for a reason.

Negative feelings often go away more quickly when *accepted* and *expressed*. When repressed feelings are not expressed verbally and openly, they become expressed in other ways. Unfortunately, these repressed feelings often resurface in the form of unhealthy mental, emotional, or physical illnesses. We can avoid discounting each other's true feelings by avoiding the use of communication roadblocks such as "yes, but ...," "should," or "shouldn't," and so forth.

The following simple technique can enhance communication through the use of "I messages." It allows the sender and receiver to understand the true feelings that often drive our behaviors, yet remain unspoken, or lost in blaming and shaming defensive responses.

I feel _____ about _____ because _____.[10]

"I *feel* sad and lonely *about* you spending so much time at work, *because* I'm worried that you enjoy your work more than you enjoy being with me."

A healthy response could utilize reflective listening to repeat back what was said in order to clarify understanding:

"You *feel* I don't love you *because* I seem more concerned with my work than with you?"

During adversity we may find ourselves irritable and impatient. If we can focus our anger and disappointments on the challenges and issues we are facing rather than each other, we are more likely to stay connected.

3. **Cooperation and Tolerance**: Many professional therapists have discovered that "Tolerance Therapy" saves more marriages than other confrontational communication-based therapies. It's difficult to "accept, not expect" in a marriage; however, most marriages do better when couples tolerate each other's differences while recognizing, focusing on, and encouraging their spouse's good qualities. It is difficult and often unproductive to focus our energies on changing our spouses. Change and growth are more likely to be realized when we focus our efforts on accepting, "receiving" (see *Receive Ye One Another,* by Larry Lewis), our spouses while positively changing ourselves.

Tolerance, cooperation, mercy, and "giving in" can break down barriers and power struggles. Larry describes the power of "going the second mile" or working from a celestial perspective which goes beyond tolerance or "giving in." In other words, I may think it only fair that my spouse come home from work, feed the kids, and help me clean up before resting on the couch. But maybe my second mile offering would be to do the work even if I have also worked a long and hard day. This principle goes beyond fairness or justice; it focuses on mercy and celestial thinking.[11]

4. **Conflict Resolution**: "Sometimes our inability to resolve conflict keeps love out of a marriage."[12] All marriages have conflicts, and not all issues can be solved easily. It is helpful to know and understand each other's family backgrounds, past losses, and personal struggles. We bring many personal issues

to our marriage. Couples may have to *agree* to *disagree* on some issues. However, some conflicts cannot be ignored. A marriage may fail over time if addictions, abuse, abandonment, or serious mental illnesses are not being addressed appropriately.

Patience and Forgiveness

Affairs pose a significant threat to marriages and families. The act of betrayal can produce a potentially devastating crisis, resulting in grief, despair, anguish, and intense anger. Many couples successfully survive this devastating crisis by utilizing marital therapy. Success is most predictable when couples care for each other and both are equally committed to making the marriage work. Attachment and bonding are vital to a secure relationship. The task in crises is finding a realistic balance between hope and reality. Couples who educate and celebrate the unique needs and differences between men and women can greatly improve their marriages.

Couples often ask how much forgiveness is required when one partner has betrayed his or her marital covenants.

> My husband got involved with another woman. It has hurt me beyond words. We are trying to save our temple marriage. He is repenting and still attends church. However, I fear I don't trust him. I wonder who he is thinking about. Does he really love me? Will he stay? Can I forgive?

The following quote adds evidence concerning the value of patience and forgiveness:

Because so many marital challenges involve a needed change of heart, repentance, and sometimes careful re-building of the relationship; partners who wait patiently through the process are a great strength and blessing to their spouses.[13]

Touch and Massage Therapy

Touch can be a healing tool. Massage therapy has been a healing art for centuries. It can bring comfort to those who are emotionally or physically ill.

Touch helps couples stay connected. Touch can dissolve anger and frustration, and melt away tension. Touch or massage therapy can, but does not have to, involve sexual intimacy in marriage. One partner may find comfort in intimacy during adversity because touch, tenderness, and intimacy may serve as a reminder that not all is lost. Others, however, may not be able to participate in physical intimacy during or immediately after a crisis. They may wonder how anyone could think of being intimate during their crisis.

The following touch technique may help bring healing and bridge the gap between partners. Couples will need to plan to be alone and undisturbed for about an hour. Realize this time together may be one of the most important exercises that can be done to sustain a relationship.

Each partner takes a turn massaging the other. Start with the back and neck, and then move onto limbs, hands, and feet.

Lotions or oils can be used if desired. Rub deep into grief-stricken muscles. Couples can talk about their concerns, or just take the time to totally relax in silence. After spending this time together, most individuals will function better emotionally and cognitively. Some couples will also notice that over time, their stress and anxiety decreases or softens.

It's also important for couples to get away and spend quality time alone together. A weekly date is worth the money and effort. Many years ago, our stake president counseled the members of our stake to borrow money for only two things: a home and a date. He also encouraged couples to spend a night away together when possible. His counsel has had a positive impact on our marriage. Communication and conflict resolution cannot occur if effort is not made to be alone together on a regular basis.

Couple's Therapy

Many couples have been helped with professional therapy. They may have developed negative or enabling behaviors or cycles that, with the help of counseling, can be altered. If couples are willing to do the work required to stay together, most marriages can become successful. Couples who want to stay together and rekindle the love they once had for each other can also benefit from couple's therapy or marital enhancement programs. Couple's therapy and marital enhancement programs and retreats help guide "the distressed couple from negative and rigidly structured responses toward flexibility and sensitive responsiveness . . . couples need."[14]

Research has shown that emotionally ill individuals can have successful marriages. Emotionally-focused therapy may be helpful. Therapists can help couples refrain from focusing on each other's weakness and teach them how to de-escalate negative cycles. Example: "I withdraw because you nag, and you nag because I withdraw." This kind of couple's therapy can help soften the blamer and help the withdrawn spouse to re-engage. An individual can move from defense and self protection to openness, where partners can become a source of security, protection, and comfort for each other. They may need help forgiving or trusting again or learning conflict resolution and communication skills. They might need to work on relationship issues and how to improve their friendship. Your bishop or local LDS Family Services can guide you to marriage counselors in your community.

When Should We Divorce?

As stated in the previous chapter, marriages impacted by chronic addictions, substance abuse, serious mental illness, physical or mental abuse, and infidelity are predictably more likely to end in divorce.[15]

Ending a marriage is usually a very difficult experience. There are some who will not have a choice.

God knows that many are suffering unfairly, often at the hand of others. God generally does not take away the agency of spouses or others who choose to harm us.

We are not required to stay indefinitely in harm's way. (See chapter one, "Abuse.") Each couple's circumstance is different and ultimately each party must be responsible to determine his own course and take responsibility for his choices and actions. God has not left us alone; inspired church leaders, LDS family service, and faithful Latter-day Saints in public and private practice can help us improve our marriages. Inspired church leaders can also provide support for those who must prayerfully determine if divorce is the best option. God has also through his Son provided the Holy Ghost to guide and comfort us, especially in those moments that we face the "but if not's" in our personal lives.

> I will not leave you comfortless: I will come to you. (John 14:18)

Notes

1. Craig H. Hart, *Helping and Healing our Families: Principles and Practices Inspired by The Family: A Proclamation to the World* (Salt Lake City: Deseret Book, 2005), 32.

2. Ibid., 39

3. Ibid., 38

4. David H. Olson, and John Defrain, *Marriage and the Family, Diversity and Strengths* (Mountain View: Mayfield Publishing, 1994).

5. M. Gamblin "Forgiveness" (lecture, Association of Mormon Counselors and Psychotherapists Conference, Salt Lake City, UT, Oct. 1997).

6. Willard F. Harley, Jr., *His Needs Her Needs: Building An Affair-proof Marriage,*

4th printing (Grand Rapids: Baker Book House, 2000), 12–13.

7. T.A. Rando "Grief" (lecture, Association for Death Education and Counseling Conference, Chicago, IL, Mar. 1998).

8. Joyce and Dennis Ashton, *Loss and Grief Recovery* (Amityville: Baywood Publishing, 1996), 116.

9. John Gray, *Talks from John Gray, author of Men are from Mars, Women are from Venus* (New York: Harper Collins, 1992).

10. The Church of Jesus Christ of Latter-day Saints Social Services Department, *Becoming a Better Parent* (Salt Lake City, 1974), 33.

11. Larry W. Lewis, *Receive Ye One another: Taking Temple Marriage the Second Mile* (Springville: Cedar Fort Inc., 2006), 55.

12. "Mending our Marriage," *Ensign*, Oct. 1996, 51.

13. Ibid.

14. Susan M. Johnson, *The practice of Emotionally Focused Couple Therapy* (New York: Brunner-Routledge, 2004), 17.

15. Diane Medved, *The Case Against Divorce: Discover the Lures, and the Emotional Traps of Divorce—Plus the Seven Vital Reasons to Stay Together,* (New York: Donald I. Fine, Inc., 1989), 121.

CHAPTER EIGHT

Unwed Pregnancies, Infertility, and Adoption

When individuals hear the word adoption, they may only picture the joy of uniting a wonderful family with a beautiful child. Few of us realize the adjustment and grief that may be a part of this joyous experience. Although we should acknowledge the joy, it is also fitting to include the impact of loss and grief when discussing the adoption process. All parties involved in an adoption will experience some symptoms of grief.

Every year, more than one million unwed pregnancies occur in Canada and the United States. Approximately 15,000 of those pregnancies involve LDS birth mothers. This averages out to be one birth mother per ward per year.[1] Whether the birth mother decides to be a single parent and raise the child herself, marry, or place the infant for adoption, it can become a stressful cascade of losses and disappointments for everyone concerned and involved.

The bereavement process often begins long before most are even aware. When the unwed biological mother discovers she is pregnant, she experiences a flood of emotions and challenges that must be addressed. Could or should she marry? Can she keep her child? Could she stay in school and support herself? Would family and friends support her decision to give her child to strangers? How will she handle her changing body image? What other changes and loss must she adjust to?

Grief experts discourage individuals from making major decisions while experiencing acute grief. Unfortunately, birth parents and adoptive applicants have limited periods of time to make major decisions that will affect their own lives and the life of the unborn child. Many of these decisions have eternal consequences.

> What do I say? It's so overwhelming. When I placed my baby for adoption, all I could think about was how much better he would be without me for a mom. I get so depressed when I think of where all this has come to (birth mother, age 16).

Birth Mothers

Statistics show that most LDS birth mothers who keep their baby and become single parents will not marry in the temple.

Those who place the child with adoptive couples are more likely to eventually marry in the temple.[2] All infants placed through LDS Family Services are sealed in the temple to their adoptive families and inherit covenant blessings.

> I can't marry right now and as hard as it seems for me to give my baby to someone else, I want him to be sealed to parents in the temple (birth mother, age 18).

> Once I became pregnant, I knew I had to become active in the church—even if I had to go by myself. I took this responsibility very seriously. I remember sitting in meetings and feeling so alone. I felt that everyone around me had this perfect happy home, married to a priesthood holder, and sealed in the temple. I didn't have this (birth mother, age 20).

Birth Fathers

When the biological father receives the news, he wonders if he should become a father to his child. Is he ready to marry and support the birth mother and a baby? What about his education and career plans? Will his friends change? What are the changes and losses he must adapt too?

> I got drunk with a friend one night. Afterwards we went to visit some girls and one of them was very aggressive and knew what she was doing. The alcohol seemed to soften my previous resistive powers. I lost my virginity. Now she thinks she is pregnant! (young man, age 18).[3]

How can I ever provide for this baby? (birth father, age 17).

Grandparents

When future grandparents of the baby receive the news, they begin to deal with their own grief, loss, and disappointment. Will their son or daughter drop out of school? Should they encourage the children to marry or place the child for adoption? Should they try to keep the pregnancy confidential? Is their child mature enough to become a parent and/or marry? How will they cope with losing a grandchild? Their grief often produces sadness, hurt, frustration, and anger.

> I can't believe my child has given up a temple marriage and a college education. My hopes for his future are shattered or at least altered. I feel hurt, angry, and afraid for him.

Adoptive couples

Adoptive couples experience loss as they confront their infertility and/or miscarriages. Often, feelings of failure, discomfort, and spiritual injury accompany them to the adoption agency.

> I worry some people have thought we were selfish because we haven't started our family. They see our new home, cars, and boat and probably wonder if that's why we have postponed having children.

> We were so thrilled to finally be pregnant! We had been in and out of fertility clinics for five years. We had finally conceived

through IUI (Intro-uterine Insemination). We were 19 weeks along and went in for our usual check up. The doctor sent us for a routine ultrasound which showed that our baby had died; we couldn't believe it! The previous week the baby had a strong heartbeat! How did this happen? Everyone around us was having children. Why us? I was in shock for days! As I anticipated being induced to deliver my baby, I still wasn't sure it was all happening. Even after delivery, I thought I could still feel the baby moving. It took a long time for me to believe I had lost my baby. My grief lasted for over a year. Most people didn't seem to understand. They claimed I never knew my child who wasn't even born yet, so why was my grief so long and so hard? I really didn't feel happy again until I was pregnant and finally delivered a healthy baby. And even now I wish I had both babies![4]

I had three ectopic pregnancies. The first one destroyed my right tube and the third one my left. The hardest part is realizing I cannot conceive again. I always just wanted to stay home and be a mom. Now I have to replan my life. I cry a lot.[5]

Grief

Most individuals within the adoption triad can intellectually understand the challenges associated with the adoption process. However, birth parents and adoptive couples considering adoption often struggle emotionally and find it hard to deal with the ongoing impact of this event in their lives. Some birth parents ask the following: "Why me?" "I'm trying to repent, why can't I handle this?" "Why am I struggling so much?" They may think: "I hope I miscarry." "What about abortion?"

Adoptive applicants enduring miscarriage and infertility ask: "Where did I go wrong?" "I have faith; I live the Gospel. Why can't I have a child?"

Parents of birth parents often endure pain as a result of the misuse of agency and poor choices of their children:

> I can't believe my son has brought all this stress into our lives.

Biological grandparents often experience fear and shame. Some of their fears include being judged negatively, especially if they feel somehow responsible for the negative choices their child has made. Their guilt can further complicate the grieving process, causing them to experience shame and a loss of control over their lives.

> Why am I having these feelings? I really must be a weak or bad person.

> No one seems to understand how hard it is to think of our grandbaby being given to another family.

Secondary Loss

Secondary loss is defined as those challenges that follow the primary event or primary loss. Secondary losses are unique to each individual in the adoptive process. For example, an unwed mother choosing adoption may have to sacrifice her education, body image, reputation, and immediate dreams of a temple marriage, in addition to mourning the loss of her child. All of these challenges, or accumulative losses combined, tend to complicate the grieving process and compromise her decision making:

> My dream of a temple marriage, college education, and the perfect body in my wedding dress are gone (birth mother, age 17).

No one involved in the adoptive process will ever be quite the same again. They see through new eyes and are forever changed as they begin to establish their "new normal."[6]

Disenfranchised Grief

When someone cannot grieve openly or others do not validate their loss, it is called disenfranchised grief. An example of this occurred some years ago when an unwed mother decided to move away from home in order to keep her pregnancy confidential. After placing her child, she moved back home and began dating a young man that had no knowledge of her pregnancy. One night he shared that he was adopted and couldn't understand why or how his mother could have "given him up?" This young woman desperately wanted to share that she knew through experience how much his mother loved him and that she had done what she felt was best for him. She wanted to share how much she loved the child she had placed with a wonderful, worthy family, and how she was giving him spiritual opportunities and a better life. She felt "she hadn't given him up, but she had actually given him more"

(LDSFS ad mantra). Unfortunately, her prior choice of confidentiality now limited her ability to help this young man. Nevertheless, her personal choice of confidentiality may have been in her best interest in the long run.

Disbelief, Denial, Shock, and Numbness

Disbelief, denial, shock, and numbness, are common emotions experienced by members of the adoption triad and their families.

> There is no way that my son is responsible for this pregnancy!

> I can't believe after 10 years of marriage and infertility that the doctors can do no more, and that God hasn't answered my pleas to get pregnant and deliver a child.

> I didn't tell anyone that I was the father because I just couldn't believe it myself!

Some individuals become unable or unwilling to acknowledge their true struggles and limitations.

> I kept my fears and feelings to myself. What would the ward think of me if they knew I couldn't handle this?

Some adoptive couples are unwilling or unable to acknowledge their pain and use avoidance patterns and denial to cope. They may consciously or unconsciously desire the biological mother to disappear after placement. Some fear if they maintain contact she may attempt to reclaim their child. This is a rare occurrence. The biological mother usually benefits from limited contact, negotiated with the adoptive couple, which allows her to know that her baby is well, happy, and keenly aware of her love. This knowledge, reassurance, and occasional contact provide confirmation to her that she has made the right decision.

Many birth fathers are consciously or subconsciously the source of additional anxiety and consternation for the birth mother. Over time, some birth mothers begin to feel it best to give their baby a home with a temple married couple. Some birth fathers agree with her plans, and unitedly they both choose adoption for their child. A smaller number of birth fathers express a sincere desire to parent the child themselves, without the birth mother's involvement. A significant number of birth fathers are unwilling to support the adoption desires of the birth mother. These same birth fathers often demonstrate little effort to assume financial responsibility and fail to actively prepare for the baby's future.

Experience has revealed that most unwed fathers who express opposition to adoption do so in attempt to maintain control or influence over the birth mother. At this stage, the potential loss of his unborn child is often a secondary loss for the birth father. The primary loss he is experiencing actually results from the ended or altered relationship between him and the birth mother, not his future relationship with the baby. His assumptive world relative to his and the birth mother's future has been assaulted or altered.

As the pregnancy progresses, the birth mother's focus changes from her and the birth father's future to her baby's future. This change in focus for many birth fathers constitutes a significant loss, resulting in increased vulnerability, anger, and attempts to control the birth mother.

Anger

Anger is a common emotion with any loss. Birth mothers often become angry with the birth father when he refuses to cooperate with her inspired and selfless plans to provide for the child through adoption. A birth mother's ability to make decisions, defuse anger, exercise control, and sacrifice for the baby's future is influenced by her own grieving processes.

Irritability is often a manifestation of anger. The mother of a pregnant young woman said:

> Since my daughter's unwed pregnancy, I don't seem to have any patience with my other children!

Anger directed towards deity or church leaders representing God is common among all religions during loss. Anger may be more intense for faithful members who believed that God should have blessed them by preventing or removing their adversity. An infertile couple lamented:

> It is hard to accept that God has allowed our infertility and multiple miscarriages. We have fasted, prayed and had

special blessings. Where is our miracle? Aren't we worthy to be parents?

I taught my child the Gospel and provided a shield for every temptation. I can't believe God allowed this and I find myself questioning if the Church is really true now that my daughter is pregnant.

Clichés

One may mean well using clichés that are intended to comfort; however, clichés can minimize a loss and suggest that someone has no legitimate need to grieve. Clichés often cause individuals to feel scrutinized and judged. Examples of well meaning yet hurtful clichés include:

You are young and will have more chances to have children, or you can always adopt a child.

Many struggle spiritually when they hear the following types of clichés:

This was God's will.

God could have prevented this if you were worthy, fasted longer, prayed more, or had more faith.

Guilt

Guilt is an emotion that is common with any adoptive placement. The adoptive parents may wonder if they are somehow responsible for their infertility and their inability to bear children. The parents of an unwed mother may wonder if there was something wrong with their parenting skills, or the spiritual direction and example in their home. Biological parents often feel guilt concerning the commandments they haven't kept, and for the situation they have put themselves and their baby in. They struggle with guilt as they try to decide to place or keep the infant. For many, guilt is the most exhausting and difficult emotion to deal with. At times, the painful consequences of prior choices become confused with the painful, yet favorable, decision to place the child for adoption.

I hurt so much when I consider placing my child for adoption.

I did so many things wrong. If I had just done things differently this wouldn't have happened.

My parents feel I should give my baby to them to raise. They don't seem to realize how hard it would be for me to see my child on a daily basis and not be involved (birth mom, age 20).

Some childless couples experience false guilt, feeling guilty for shortcomings and imperfections in their lives that they now attribute to their infertility.

If I had lived a better life, or exercised more faith, I wouldn't be infertile now.

Vulnerability and Loss of Control

Feeling vulnerable and out of control is a common reaction with the unwed mother placing her infant. She fears she will never know how the child is doing and if she made the right choice. She is often comforted by her decision to place if the adoptive couple can reassure her periodically that her child is doing well and will grow up knowing of her love.

The adoptive couple feels more control when they finally receive their baby; however, their vulnerability and accompanying need for control may cause them to resist the biological mother's attempts to find meaning, purpose, and peace in her adoption decision through ongoing periodic contact. Some adoptive couples reason:

> What if the biological mom wants more information so she can come looking for her child?

> We are hesitant to share the very best pictures of our adoptive son with his birth mother, because we fear seeing the pictures will make her want him back.

This is a frightening task for the adoptive couple; however, their willingness to give information and support actually calms the vulnerability, grief, and loss of control the unwed mother is feeling. The likelihood of her rescinding her decision is lessened when she is given sufficient feedback and reassurance that allows her to "feel and heal."

All of the above emotional reactions can stress the body, causing physical reactions. The physical symptoms may include breathlessness, restlessness, palpitations, headaches, fatigue, and changes in appetite, sleep, bowels, or sexual desire.

> After years of infertility and 6 months after losing our baby I started having lots of unusual physical symptoms. The doctors did some tests and concluded my physical problems were a result of all that I had been through emotionally. I had a lot of anxiety.

It may be difficult to concentrate on anything except what has happened. This preoccupation can lead to absent-mindedness, ruminations, confusion, and disorganization for an extended period of time. When trying to make some sense of what has occurred, one may repeatedly ask the same questions over and over again.

> I go over and over what happened the night I got pregnant. I think about all the decisions that led me to this point in my life.

This mental repetition (rumination) is a desperate attempt to consider other solutions that could have altered the outcome. An infertile couple questioned, "What if I had attempted to conceive earlier?" or "What if we had gone to the doctor sooner, would I have miscarried?"

The biological mother thinks, "If I hadn't dated him, I wouldn't be pregnant now."

The biological grandparents ask themselves what they could have done differently to have prevented the situation. They all may mentally search for a different and or better conclusion, diagnosis, or prognosis. They try to regain some control by re-creating or replaying aspects of their experience.

Some have feelings of being scrutinized and judged. An infertile couple said, "People have asked why we have such a big house with no children."

Others experience a loss of friends, which causes changes in roles and identity.

> My friends, work associates and everyone in the ward seems to be judging our parenting skills since our daughter became pregnant.

> I feel like I am under glass, people keep staring at me since they heard I am pregnant, looking at my stomach to see if I've gotten bigger.

It may be confusing for those who have strong faith, believe in miracles, and are striving to live the gospel, when they feel they were not protected or shielded from such a serious trial.

> I thought if I lived the commandments I would conceive and become a mother someday.

Finding Meaning

The most common question in the adoption process may be,

"Why?" It may be "Why me?" "Why medically?" or "Why, God?"
An infertile couple wonders why medically they cannot conceive
or why God has not blessed them with children. The grandparents
of an unborn child wonder why they are in this difficult position.
The "why's" are difficult to answer. Generally, individuals must
find their own why's as they discover meaning in their unique situations. Some find meaning through the spiritual interventions
of prayer, revelation, impressions, scripture reading, church and
temple attendance, or dreams. We may take these interventions
for granted as church members because they have always been
available. Finding meaning for the unwed mother might be the
confirmation from God that she is to keep her infant or place the
child with loving, eager parents.

> I feel that placing my baby with a father and mother is the
> best thing for my child (25-year-old college student).

A spiritual confirmation helps her find purpose and solace. A
similar confirmation for both sets of grandparents and the birth
father is often beneficial. Hearing, contemplating, and praying
for personal confirmation are never easy tasks. Some have found
comfort in the following counsel from the First Presidency's 2002
letter to Church leaders concerning unwed parents:

> When a man and woman conceive a child out of wedlock,
> every effort should be made to encourage them to marry. When
> the probability of a successful marriage is unlikely due to age

or other circumstances, unwed parents should be counseled to place the child for adoption through LDS Family Services to ensure that the baby will be sealed to temple-worthy parents. Adoption is an unselfish, loving decision that blesses both the birth parents and the child in this life and in eternity.

Birth parents who do not marry should not be counseled to keep the infant as a condition of repentance or out of a sense of obligation to care for one's own. Unwed parents are not able to provide the blessings of the sealing covenant. Further, they are generally unable to provide a stable, nurturing environment which is so essential for the baby's well-being. Unmarried parents should give prayerful consideration to the best interests of the child and the blessings that can come to an infant who is sealed to a mother and father.[7]

President Spencer W. Kimball gave similar direction in 1976. While speaking concerning abortion, he provided the first recorded counsel relative to unmarried parents:

Often the question is asked, what should unmarried parents do then? Whenever possible, unwed parents should marry and build a home. When this is not possible, adoption through Church Social Services is preferred so that the infant can be sealed to loving eager parents in an eternal family. A baby needs a family, a father and a mother. The Lord intended for babies to have a family and for families to be eternal.[8]

For members of the adoption triad, the inspired counsel of living prophets confirms that God can bless each life as we turn to him, even in the midst of our darkest despair.

Both my daughter and I had a powerful spiritual confirmation that the baby she was carrying should be placed with a mother and father who could have the baby sealed to them in the temple. The peace that we both felt is what helped me let go of my grandchild and avoid additional feelings of pain and grief. (maternal grandfather)

I felt I should keep my baby and live worthy of a husband and temple marriage later. (birth mother, age 18)

Professionals suggest it may take 24 months or more to adjust to loss and major changes in our lives.[9] See *But If Not ... Volume I* for additional coping and healing interventions.

Notes

1. Dennis Ashton and Dr. Cyril Figuere, LDS Family Services statistics, 1995.

2. Ibid.

3. Joyce and Dennis Ashton, *Jesus Wept* (Springville, Utah: Cedar Fort Inc., 2002), 44.

4. Ibid, 25.

5. Ibid, 26.

6. R. K. Limbo and S. R. Wheeler, *When a Baby Dies: A handbook for Healing and Helping* (La Crosse: Resolve Through Sharing, 1986), xv.

7. First Presidency (letter), June 26, 2002, Gordon B. Hinckley, Thomas S. Monson, and James E. Faust

8. Spencer W. Kimball, *A Visit from the Prophet*, WOF1420.

9. Glen W. Davidson, *Understanding Mourning* (Minneapolis: Augsburg Publishing House, 1982), figures 1–4.

CHAPTER NINE

Same-gender Attraction, Aging, and Empty Nest

Same-gender attraction is an intense interest in others of the same sex, usually leading to sexual desire. However, it often has less to do with sexuality, and more to do with the need for love, affection, and acceptance from the same gender. Experts are divided on cause; however most agree that both biology and environment play a role. Dr. Dean Byrd, PhD, an expert in the field, feels that biology plays a part in all behavior; however, homosexuality is more a derailing of biological priming. He feels there are multi-determined causes and many different factors for different individuals. There are childhood events and environmental factors. Note that it is common for children to have sexual exploration with little friends of the same gender. Homosexuality occurs if they don't turn when they are older and have a need for intimacy from the opposite sex. One may be predispositioned rather than predetermined. Nature and nurture play complex roles.[1] Here are a few common factors:

1.   A child may have had an early introduction to sex by someone of the same sex. In fact where sexual abuse has occurred by someone of the same sex, same-gender attraction is 7 times more common.[2] (Find interventions for coping with abuse in *But if Not* . . . Volume I; also see 2 Nephi 2.)

2.   A child may not have felt loved or supported by their same-sex parent. As they try to fill the void through supportive and loving friends of the same gender, sometimes reinforced sexual feelings may result as they address their emotional needs.

Elder Neal Maxwell teaches, "Our genes, circumstances. and environment matter very much and they shape us very much, yet there remains an inner zone. In this zone lies the essence of our individuality and our personal accounts."[3]

The 2000 census data reports that 594,391 same-sex couples reported living together in the United States. In 2005 it grew to 777,000. The 30 percent increase may be due to couples being more willing to report accurately; 53 percent were two men living together and 47 percent women. For the 2010 report, the census bureau has decided to use new methods for reporting, as some states have legalized same-sex marriage. The 2005 census figures show that Utah has 3,370 self-reporting households. It is estimated that 2 to 4 percent of the LDS population experience same-gender attraction.[4]

It is also estimated that over 2 million heterosexual marriages include a gay spouse. Some same-sex attracted individuals live alone, never marrying or practicing their homosexuality.

Some LDS same-gender attracted individuals choose to marry in the temple and live heterosexual lives, bearing and parenting children. Many have testimonies of the restored gospel and desire desperately to lose their attraction to individuals of their same gender. Others are sitting among us in sacrament meetings, holding and loving their children, yet feeling hurt and lonely because they believe few can or will ever understand their anger, grief, pain, and confusion.

President Gordon B. Hinckley offers compassion and important counsel:

> Our hearts reach out to those who refer to themselves as gays and lesbians. We love and honor them as sons and daughters of God. They are welcome in the Church. It is expected, however, that they follow the same God-given rules of sexual conduct that apply to everyone. . . . The Church's opposition to attempts to legalize same-sex marriage should never be interpreted as justification for hatred, intolerance, or abuse of those who profess homosexual tendencies.[5]

Listen to the struggle of this LDS man as he tries to make sense of his life experiences.

I was sexually abused as a child. I remember thinking when I was to be ordained a deacon that I could become "clean". I talked about it with my bishop, seeking a worthy feeling. I was active in the church and fulfilled my priesthood responsibilities. I served an honorable mission. Although I struggled with masturbation at times, I was determined to overcome my problem. I married a wonderful, spiritual woman in the LDS temple. We have several children. I have undergone years of therapy through LDS Family Services. I had many counseling hours with bishops and stake presidents. However, after children and many years of marriage we are divorcing because of my homosexuality. Now I wonder if I didn't pray hard enough. I wonder if I didn't study enough. I wonder if I gave up. Did I give it my all?[6]

The loss and grief issues emerging from homosexual lifestyles are significant, not only for the same-sex attracted individual, but also for extended family members and friends that are left wondering why their circumstances are not different.

A divorced member said:

I thought my husband would be able to overcome his homosexuality. He served a mission and married me in the temple. I love him and want him forever. However we have decided on divorce because he cannot function in the marriage. He is not sexually attracted to me. It is very painful to suffer such an eternal loss. I sometimes feel like a failure and don't want to give up. However, after all the prayers, blessings, fasting, and therapy, he hasn't changed. I think his natural death would be an easier solution. At least I would know I could have him in the eternities.[7]

After much fasting and prayer I felt impressed to marry a certain returned missionary. Little did I know that many years later he would leave for his homosexual lifestyle. Most of my children have suffered intensely from the divorce. Many have left the church, which breaks my heart.

Some same-gender attracted people receive healing or control over their same-sex attraction, others do not. It is a painful and disappointing challenge for them and their families.

A former missionary writes:

I feel like I have no choice but to either do it [recover from his same sex attraction] or live my life with a guilty conscience that would eventually drive me crazy. It is so painful to feel different, guilty, and desperate. The shame and unacceptance I feel at church is making me bitter. I'm not sure I can keep going there. I've fasted, prayed, done it all. Sometimes suicide seems the only way out . . . it seems a good option at times.

A man struggling with same-sex attraction writes:

I have done everything, the counseling, bishop and stake president meetings, prayer, support groups, sports, reading, and so forth. The only hope I see at this point is a miracle. As I weigh things out in my mind, it seems only logical and right that we should get divorced for my wife's sake. However, there is a great deal to fear: the effect on our children, financial devastation, and loss of self-esteem. Could I handle losing my family eternally? On the other hand, I would feel some relief, a decision would be made and I would be able to stop feeling like I have to pretend and cover up my real feelings. What do I do?[8]

Offering treatment to same-gender attracted individuals is controversial. The professional world is torn, not only on the cause, but the treatment of homosexuality. Many professionals feel that offering treatment wrongly suggests that an individual can change his or her sexual orientation. Yet many who suffer want to change the attraction. Seeking the right professional therapist then becomes critical for those who desire to change or find a way to deal with their attraction. Dr. Dean Bryd says that interpersonal processes can modify biology and that de-sexualizing the attraction can soften same-gender attraction.[9]

Ty Mansfield, author of *In Quiet Desperation: Understanding the Challenge of Same Gender Attraction*, said, "I know some individuals who feel they have overcome the attraction, have married, and it's not a problem for them anymore. ... I know many more who have the type of life they want—married with a family. They still experience the attraction, but that's all they see it as."[10]

The Church and LDS Family Services support Evergreen International (an LDS-based program) and other organizations that provide hope for those who desire to change. Reparative therapy has helped many in their difficult struggle. The Church of Jesus Christ of Latter-day Saints' position is defined clearly in The Family: A Proclamation to the World.

The proclamation encourages the abstaining of any sexual

involvement outside of marriage, whether in heterosexual or homosexual relationships. Those struggling with homosexuality and sexual addictions generally need to stop the behavior before they can successfully address the psychological and spiritual aspects of their challenges.

Self-referral to LDS Family Services

Historically, pregnant unmarried women and individuals seeking help with homosexual issues have been able to confidentially refer themselves to LDS Family Services. Others have accessed services through a bishop's referral. However, to reduce administrative demands of bishops and encourage individuals to be self-reliant in solving personal problems, individuals may now refer themselves to LDS Family Services in addition to choosing other community resources for therapy. Bishops may also continue to refer members to LDS Family Services.

Individuals who desire assistance from fast offerings to pay for this service are to make such arrangements with the bishop before referral to LDS Family Services. Bishops will be consulted regarding the client's progress when the client has signed a release of information allowing such information to be shared with the bishop.

Never Married

For individuals who desire to marry and don't, it can be a

terrible disappointment and loss. Some well-meaning friends remind singles that theirs is not an eternal loss, explaining that they will find a spouse in the next life. However, this counsel does not recognize or allow them to mourn and grieve for all they don't have here and now.

> I always thought I would marry someday and bear children. However, I am now nearing menopause and the hope of a family is fading. Everyone reminds me that I am promised a family someday . . . I guess in the next life, but I feel sad and gypped now.

Other Types of Losses

Another change we may underestimate is the impact of retirement and employment changes. The following is from a woman who lost a job she had enjoyed for 25 years.

> I miss the old way—I miss the old friends! I haven't written that grief letter about my feelings, but I do think and cry about it daily, and I am going to write it soon and hope it helps me feel better.

Empty Nest

It has been a few short months since we cared for our sweet mother in our home with the help of hospice and family. Three weeks after Mother died, our youngest daughter married. We miss having both of these great women in our home, and have discovered that even joyful events require adjustments. A few weeks following Ashley's marriage, our youngest son Brandon moved from our home to attend medical school in a different state. When we were raising five children, (one in a wheelchair) we were always busy and felt overwhelmed at times. Our young family (full nest) brought challenges, fun, and blessing. Now our empty nest family creates an equally challenging adjustment.

A close friend saying goodbye to her married daughter describes her empty nest well.

> "I know how hard it is to have a daughter get married—with my first it was so very painful! I still miss them and it can't really ever be the same. How can you raise her and teach and love her so much and then just give her to someone else? So not fair!"

One day after cleaning out my mother's home following her death, I had what I call a "grief attack." I sent the following email to all my friends and family. I wanted anyone and everyone to offer me their comfort and advice. It really helped to share my feelings and then receive back love and support.

> "I am still struggling with the fact that both of my parents are dead and now I am the "old grandma generation" and I am probably the next one to die . . . it's really weird . . . I look in the mirror and see an older face whose life could be almost over!! . . . And cleaning out Mom's house is sad and draining.

Now, months later, I realize after reading those feelings, how much better I am doing. It is a testament of how the human soul can adjust to the losses that come our way. We are resilient; we can find peace, hope, and happiness again, in spite of our life's challenges. Life is worth living, and though things will never be quite the same, most of us can find meaning as we discover our new normal.

Our New Loss: Aging

Life is full of change, loss, and adjustment. We have thought of including aging as a loss and something that many individuals grieve for. Now that Dennis and I are young senior citizens we are trying to find ways to adapt as our bodies decline. I also work with hospice patients who are most often 65 years and older. I listen to their struggles and losses as their bodies fail and they prepare for death. Many have suffered for years, while others have a quicker death. Patients tell me how difficult it is to first give up sports, jogging, and then even walking. For some, these loses will be followed by the loss of their driver's licenses and having to move out of the homes they love. I realize more fully that by the time we die we have to give up everything earthly.

Soon after Dennis and I experienced the death of our last parent, combined with our last child leaving home, I started experiencing some new physical struggles. I knew from past experience and research that bereaved individuals are vulnerable and often experience a decline in their physical health. Grief can affect us emotionally, spiritually, as well as physically (see *Jesus Wept*). I tried to keep my humor as I felt my body was falling apart, but I will admit it was frightening, and sad at times for me.

These events and losses brought about the reality and limits of our "new normal." We have felt the vulnerability of aging that includes joining the old generation. In the mean time, I will have to learn to focus on other interests and try to be grateful for the many things I can still do. This Pearl Buck quote about accepting her mentally disabled child has been a favorite for years:

> Only to endure is not enough. Endurance can be a harsh and bitter root in one's life, bearing poisonous and gloomy fruit, destroying other's lives. Endurance is only the beginning. There must be acceptance and the knowledge that sorrow fully accepted brings its own gifts.[11]

I know God can heal us physically, emotionally, and mentally, "but if not . . . ," we will continue to believe, have faith in God, and endure to the end.

"Grief becomes your companion and teacher as you learn to live with it."[12]

"My philosophy of life is that it's like being on a beach. You get knocked down by a wave and you can either lie there and drown, or you can get up and move. If you don't keep moving you die."[13]

For the Wounded

We are all likely to be wounded at sometime in our life. We must remember Christ's example when he appeared in the

America's, He invited those present to touch the wounds in his hands and feet (not his strong, healthy biceps[14]). Those present experienced firsthand the wounds and pain the Savior suffered for them. He is connected to them and to us through his suffering. We too can connect to others through our own suffering.

We have not been left without the Savior's comfort. Those same wounds represent healing for each of us as we earnestly seek the Savior's Atonement in our lives. May God bless you on your journey.

Notes

1. Dr. Dean Byrd, "Providing Psychological Care to Men Who Present with Unwanted Homosexual Attraction: An Interpersonal Approach" (lecture, Association of Mormon Counselors and Psychotherapists Conference, Salt Lake City, Oct. 3, 2008).

2. Ibid.

3. Neal A. Maxwell, "According to the Desire of [Our] Hearts," *Ensign*, Nov. 1996, 21.

4. Ogden Standard-Examiner, Jun. 11, 2005, 1A.

5. Carrie A. Moore, "Alone in the fold: Many LDS gays struggle to cling to faith despite their yearnings," *Deseret Morning News*, Dec. 3, 2005.

6. Joyce and Dennis Ashton, *Jesus Wept* (Springville, Utah: Cedar Fort, Inc., 2001), 51

7. Ibid, 52.

8. Ibid., 53.

9. Dr. Dean Byrd, "Providing Psychological Care to Men Who Present with Unwanted Homosexual Attraction: An Interpersonal Approach."

10. Moore, "Alone in the fold: Many LDS gays struggle to cling to faith despite their yearnings."

11. P. S. Buck, *The Child Who Never Grew* (Bethesda: Woodbine House, 1950), 25.

12. D. Edwards, *Grieving: The Pain and the Promise* (Salt Lake City: Covenant, 1989), vii.

13. Robin Simons, *After The Tears* (Orlando: Harcourt Brace Jovanovich, 1985), 8.

14. Terrence C. Smith, "An Anatomy of Troubles" (lecture, Association of Mormon Counselors and Psychotherapists Conference, Salt Lake City, Oct. 3, 2008).

ABOUT THE AUTHORS

Joyce Ashton is a registered nurse and certified bereavement advisor. She is currently the Director of Spiritual Care for Rocky Mountain Hospice.

Dennis is a licensed clinical social worker, former bishop, and assistant commissioner for LDS Family Services. He is currently the agency director for the LDS Family Services Centerville-Layton Utah agencies. Dennis was a guest on KRNS and KSL following the Salt Lake City Trolley Square shooting and Crandall Canyon Mine disaster. He has also appeared on *Living Essentials*.

Joyce and Dennis teach at BYU Education Week and have been broadcast on KBYU-TV. They have authored four other books, *Jesus Wept*, *Loss and Grief Recovery*, *But if Not* Volume I, and *But if Not* Volume II, and they have published online and journal articles.

Joyce and Dennis are the parents of six children, four of whom are living, and have several grandchildren.